Business Strategy Success Principles

BUSINESS STRATEGY SUCCESS PRINCIPLES

*An Action Plan to Grow Your Business
and Enjoy an Easier Life*

PAUL ARNOLD

NEW YORK

LONDON • NASHVILLE • MELBOURNE • VANCOUVER

Business Strategy Success Principles

An Action Plan to Grow Your Business and Enjoy an Easier Life

Published in New York, New York, by Morgan James Publishing. Morgan James is a trademark of Morgan James, LLC. www.MorganJamesPublishing.com

Proudly distributed by Ingram Publisher Services.

A FREE ebook edition is available for you or a friend with the purchase of this print book.

CLEARLY SIGN YOUR NAME ABOVE

Instructions to claim your free ebook edition:
1. Visit MorganJamesBOGO.com
2. Sign your name CLEARLY in the space above
3. Complete the form and submit a photo of this entire page
4. You or your friend can download the ebook to your preferred device

ISBN 9781631957949 paperback
ISBN 9781631957956 ebook
Library of Congress Control Number:
2021920823

Cover Design by:
Rachel Lopez
www.r2cdesign.com

Interior Design by:
Christopher Kirk
www.GFSstudio.com

Morgan James is a proud partner of Habitat for Humanity Peninsula and Greater Williamsburg. Partners in building since 2006.

Get involved today! Visit MorganJamesPublishing.com/giving-back

Contents

Acknowledgments

I t was an enormous task creating this book. I couldn't have completed it without the support of my family. To my wife, Beverly, for your endless patience and for keeping everything operating at home while I was absorbed in writing this book. To my girls, Micaela and Madelyn, for keeping me inspired with lots of love and affection. To my mother, Carynne, who provide endless support for my various endeavors and my father, Dr. Stephen Arnold, for providing the first edit of my book. To my sister, Caroline, and the Petznick family for the fun and memories. You continue to be in my thoughts and prayers!

I must give credit to the Ottawa business community. I have gained both knowledge and inspiration for this book from countless networking events attended in the National Capital Region. Entrepreneurs include my photographer Stacey Stewart, my video editor and model Candice Fraser, and my solid networking buddies Jeremy DeMerchant, Mark Granada, Jason Petrunik, and Drew Masaro who made the networking business more fun! I appreciate marketing experts Kensel Tracey and Mitch Proulx who provided much knowledge and expertise through several interviews. To all my Toastmaster entrepreneurs including Amanda Lee, Paul Newton, Cindy Little, Karen Stillman, Camille Ferland, Lorrie Brown, and Steph Wise who provided personal development to improve public speaking. Thanks to the other entrepreneurial community builders including Emile Salem and the Collab Space team, Jarrod Goldsmith, Dylan Black, Rouba Fattal, and Janet Seto.

Important content for this book came from the successful entrepreneurs I interviewed including Bruce Linton, W. Brett Wilson, and JT Foxx. James MacNeil and Jack Canfield have also been important role models for me with their work in communication, mindset, and visualization. Special mention to Steve Cody who continues to impress with new successful business ventures. Important to acknowledge is the guidance I received for this book from Ken Dunn and Nicholas Boothman, who helped me craft my book. I made new connections through the book writing workshop including Martin Wales, Amy Scruggs, and Dr. Stacey CooperLatimer.

I wanted to thank those who have contributed knowledge and expertise to the Adapt & Overcome events including Tanys Coughlan, Lana Burnley, Darpan Ahluwalia, Brian Tohana, Emily Pilon, Dr. Tatyana Lachowich, Lesley Moll, Majeed Mogharreban, Micheal Pacitto, Kru Mel Bellissimo, Laurie-ann Sheldrick and Will Pearl. A&O was taken to the next level with my fabulous co-host Shannon Ferguson and VA Andrea Ovalle. Special thanks to Jennifer Grace Hill and Stephen Whiteley for the photo and boating adventure. Thanks to my business coach Michael Charles who has given me a wealth of knowledge, guidance, and expertise through my entrepreneurial journey.

Last but certainly not least, I must give special thanks to the Morgan James Publishing family for bringing this book to life. David Hancock gave me full confidence to make this book a reality. Special thanks also to Margo, James, Margaret, and Aubrey for guiding me through the complex journey of publishing. Thanks to Arsalan from Fiverr for formatting the worksheets. Lastly, I need to recognize my editor Aubrey Kosa of Tangling Words for improving my words, formatting my book, and completing the finishing touches on *Business Strategy Success Principles*!

Introduction
Why Should You Read This Book?

L aunching a new business and finding success can be a difficult task. As entrepreneurs, we often reach a point where we
feel stuck. Our business becomes stagnant; we lose motivation and cannot grow our business as fast as we would like. In this
book, we will explore the most important strategies to run and grow
a successful business.

The first step is to understand the top five reasons most businesses fail and make sure you don't repeat any of these mistakes. We
will discuss the fundamental principles of how to grow a successful business by improving focus, efficiency, and strategy. Once you
incorporate these strategies into your business, it will allow you to
free up more time and enjoy an easier life to ultimately have more
fun in your business.

We will examine the essential elements of your business plan,
starting with the intrinsic value of your product or service. We discuss the fundamentals principles of your business plan, including
your mission statement, SWOT analysis, financial goals, and tar-

gets. We examine important tools you will need to get your business running at its full potential. We discuss the importance of having a strong brand by using strategic communication. We look at the importance of building the right team and surrounding yourself with the right people. We discuss important strategies you need to take your business to the next level and reach your fullest potential.

It is also critical to understand the importance of mindset. Having an optimistic growth mindset is essential to creating a successful business by connecting to your personal "Why." We will review how to create a vision board using inspirational images and words to affirm your future life's vision to manifest your ideal life. Then we discuss the importance of having fun and finding enjoyment in your business. By following these principles, you can operate more effectively in front of your clients and grow faster by creating a referable business.

After experiencing the global pandemic that began in 2020, it is important to understand how to adapt and overcome changes in the economy and business. I included a special section on how to properly execute a change strategy while reducing risk to ensure your business remains profitable. This is the same process that Fortune 500 companies use.

After reading *Business Strategy Success Principles*, you will understand how to grow your business faster by focusing on what is important. You will learn how to improve your business strategy to become unstoppable. By working smarter and not harder, you are able to grow your business revenue and free up time to enjoy an easier life.

It is not all about the hustle to create a successful business. It is about making the most of your time and finding enjoyment in what you do. By expanding your growth mindset, improving focus, systems, and strategy, you can make more money while working less.

I have also chosen to share some personal successes and failures that I have experienced in business. I am sharing these so you can learn from my mistakes. These are mistakes that I have learned from and used as motivation to become better, improve my education, and learn the art and science of creating a sound business strategy. I will also share some best practices from interviews I have had with multimillionaire entrepreneurs, including Bruce Linton, JT Foxx, and W. Brett Wilson.

PART 1:
YOUR PLAN

1. Should I?

Do You Have a Solid Business?

Don't Fall into One of These Five Traps

The first step to improving your business is to understand why businesses fail and don't fall into any of those traps. According to the 2018 Forbes Finance Council study, 20 percent of businesses fail after one year, 50 percent by year five, and 65 percent by year ten. The top five reasons businesses fail are as follows.

1. No need in the market: nobody wants what you are selling.
2. Not enough capital: one-quarter of business owners say they aren't able to obtain the funds they need to operate their business; there is not much you can do if your business does not have sufficient capital to operate.
3. Not the right team: either they had no partner to balance them out or the founding team could not find the right person to launch the business.

4. Competition: in some businesses, such as technology, there is a lot of competition; while it is important to be aware of your competition, one must avoid being obsessed with or run down by it.
5. Price: if you price your product too high, you'll push customers away, and if you price it too low, you won't be able to turn a profit.

Understanding the top reasons businesses fail can help you learn valuable lessons to position you and your business for a greater likelihood of success. Employing these principles into your business will enable you to create a six-figure business in less than five years. Once you are established, you can further refine the systems, strategies, and focus to double revenue, free up time, and create the business of your dreams. To build your perfect business, follow these principles. It is also important to have an accountability partner to inspire you and achieve success. An accountability partner can either be a business coach or consultant. You can also use a group accountability team, such as a mastermind or business club.

Is It a Good Idea?

Take a step back and do not fall into the number one trap for why businesses fail, which is to create a product or service for which there is no market need. Before you launch your wonderful business and focus hours upon hours on growing your business, let's step back to examine your product or service. Often, we become enamored with our idea and want to invest all of our time and money into promoting our business venture.

We imagine that others will see our beautiful business just as we see it in our own eyes. The fact is that everyone else is busy in their own lives, facing their own problems. Ultimately, they will only invest capital in your product or service if you have a sound business brand they know, like, and trust—that can benefit them personally.

I encourage you to step back at first. Try to find someone in the same field or a similar business and discuss your concept with them. I am not suggesting giving all your trade secrets away. I want you to hear from another's perspective. Most business owners would be flattered to be asked for advice and would be happy to share their ideas on the viability of a similar product or service. Even for established business owners, feedback will only help you improve by gaining a qualified outside perspective.

There could be excessive costs to market your product in a competitive industry. If you are trying to launch an energy drink or new clothing line, you will be up against companies with million-dollar marketing budgets and mass production. If you are launching a personal training business, you will also be up against established national gyms and personal trainers. You want to make sure you have done a reality check to examine the viability of your product or service to ensure success.

Watch some episodes of *Dragons' Den* or *Shark Tank*. Examine episodes where the entrepreneur is trying to launch a board game or an energy drink. The first problem is these people usually think their idea is worth ten times more than can be proven through sales. They usually have unrealistic expectations of potential buyers of their product. They may not have sufficiently examined their competition.

An entrepreneur may launch a board game without considering Hasbro: an established board game corporation now modernizing classic games like Monopoly and Game of Life. If you are starting an energy drink, you are going to up against Coca-Cola and Pepsi, which already have established billion-dollar brands and distribution. However, if you are launching a beverage with the ultimate goal to sell your company to Coca-Cola or Pepsi, you are on the right track!

My First Bad Idea

When I launched my first business, I wanted to work as an electronic music promoter. I learned some important lessons and consequences of not understanding the market. I loved going out to these three-to-four-day electronic music festivals and meeting these free-minded, rainbow-gathering, hippy people. I discovered new artists and new music sounds that stimulated my temporal mind. I loved the tribal visceral rhythms. I would dance through the night while feeling free-spirited in this tribal community.

In my early twenties, I had the ill-informed idea to start my own music promotion event company called Spectrum Music. The first problem was that I lived in a small city of about 100,000 people that would not support an individual music promotion company. The second thing I didn't realize was that the underground drug dealers make their living from these types of events.

I learned a hard lesson after I had kicked a drug dealer out one event. That same individual ruined my reputation, which negatively affected the turnout at my next event. The third mistake I made was growing too fast, too soon. I convinced my parents to cosign on a loan so I could hire and fly an international group to my small city of Kingston.

It was also a miserable experience, and I had a horrible time at the event. I had people show up at the event assuming that I was lying about these international artists performing in our small town. I had to arrange for a friend to drive all the way to Toronto to pick them up. The security team I agreed to provide, which included the local ski patrol, did not even show up except for one guy I woke up in the middle of the night and convinced to attend. I had to call my parents in the middle of the night to become my new security detail. The performers hardly made it through customs, and, luckily, I was guided in my response to the border custom officials.

The company that provided the visuals (which I learned after had included some pornography) forced me to drive to my bank and pay them after I had no money left at the event sales. I ran out of funds to pay the artist the full amount after paying for their flights. I wrote them a check for the balance, which I had no intention of honoring. My justification for not paying them more was simple: I had already paid for their flights, and they had gigged an extra night in New York on my dime without consulting me.

I ended up in about $5,000 in debt, which took me a few years to pay off. This event was also a miserable experience as I was stressed the whole evening. I had every vendor asking me for money. I was flying by the seat of my pants and paying vendors in cash as we made money from the canteen. Lesson learned: understand the market need and environment before launching a business. It is better to identify market opportunities and threats ahead of time before you invest too much time or energy into your business. The easiest way to do this is by creating a business plan.

2. Why Do This?
Plan Your Destination

What is Your Mission?

Your mission statement defines your business, your business goals, and strategies to achieve objectives. Start with defining what your product or service is in layman's terms.

The first step is to define your product or service without sounding "salesy" or marketing. For a financial advisor, you sell investment products, including stocks, bonds, GICs, mutual funds, and exchange-traded funds. For a realtor, your product is residential homes or commercial real estate.

The next step is to define the service or value you provide to your clients and figure out what differentiates you from everyone else in your market. What is the reason someone would do business with you, your product, or your service rather than doing it themselves?

Typically, the biggest differentiator is **you**!

For example:

A. For a financial advisor, your service may include retirement plans, estate plans, and investment strategies.
B. Services for a realtor would be buying or selling your home. It could also include providing a local market analysis on the area where you are buying or selling. It could be a marketing strategy, including local listings, open houses or virtual viewings, and direct marketing to other realtors.

Ultimately the differentiator is the purpose and objective related to your customer needs and team values. You want to define your target market here and the end goal of your business. Do you help established business owners manage recruiting and human resources? Do you help women ages twenty-five to fifty-five get more fit and healthy through a structured diet and innovative exercise routine? You should have a specific target market. If you can't be specific at the start, strive to define your target market in your second year after you experiment with several profitable target markets.

Your mission statement describes where you want to be and how you will get there. You want to define what the ultimate goal is that you want to achieve. Maybe that is to have your own real estate team. Maybe you want to be a leader in your community and help first-time home buyers find their dream home.

What is Your Vision?

Your vision statement describes the desired future position of your company. Your vision is the ultimate goal of what your business will accomplish. It can be combined with a mission to state the business purpose, goals, and values. Create your vision of your business, where you want to be in five, ten, and twenty years.

For example:

A. By 2040, my business will serve three hundred family households of $100 million in assets and support the local little league baseball league.

B. As a couple's relationship coach, I want to service two hundred family households, improving communication and listening strategies to improve intimacy and wellbeing. I will be a leader in my community and be an expert in improving relationships. I will do this by improving communication between couples and reducing the divorce and separation rates.

Revisit Your Mission Each Year

When a composer is creating a symphony, there are three main sections: the exposition, development and recapitulation. When Beethoven was composing "Symphony No. 5" and he was expressing his notion of fate as he learned that he was losing his hearing, he had the fundamental idea of the three repeated notes that end on a lower note a minor third below. He had an overall framework of the piece, including the main theme, development, and recapitulation (return of the theme) with the fate note theme used throughout.

By having a structure to his symphony, he was able to eventually create his "Symphony No. 9" without hearing. Despite the terrible tragedy of losing his hearing, he still overcame this obstacle because he had a plan. His "Symphony No. 9" became one of his greatest works and was performed during the tearing down of the Berlin Wall separating East and West Germany.

You need to do the same thing in business. You may have a powerful core product or service. You can improvise your way through your business, or you can start with a framework. You should have an overall plan and mission to your business so that you can stay on the right course and achieve the objective for your business. Ask yourself: Why is my product or service going to change people's lives for the better? Why should someone buy it? Why would they want my service over someone else's?

At least once a year, revisit your business plan and determine if your business has changed or if it is time to change and adapt to the market. The world may have changed to deal with a global pandemic, and you need to realign your vision and mission statement. Going through economic challenges like September 11, the 2008 mortgage crises, or the COVID-19 pandemic forced many businesses to change or pivot their business or risk extinction. Many established retailers that relied on store traffic are going extinct and facing insolvency because of the pandemic and global shutdown.

Your business plan helps you stay focused in accordance with your mission. Ultimately you may want to make the world a better place than how you left it. If the world changes, will you be able to adapt to this change and overcome these unforeseen obstacles?

You should not keep manufacturing CDs or cassette tapes when people are buying music online. Stay present and adapt your business to the changing landscape. Walt Disney started off with cartoons and a Disney playland. They have now launched an online Disney platform to compete with Netflix. If you cannot compete with changes in technology, then partner with someone else who can. Understand what your strengths are and hire to your weakness.

Here are six reasons why it is essential to have a vision and mission statement for your business:

1. Vision and mission statements define the purpose of an organization. They give a sense of identity and belonging to the employees. In turn, this helps motivate employees to achieve more success in their job.

2. It provides a "North Star" goal for the organization and gives a clear sense of direction where it is going. This allows the business to focus on an objective that it is striving to achieve.

3. Having a focus mission statement helps align the resources of an enterprise toward a successful future.

4. The mission statement provides the owner or management with a clear and effective guide when it comes to making important decisions. The vision statement provides the direction so that any decisions will align with the long-term goals.

5. The vision and mission statement help to align all the staff of an organization. This in turn increases efficiency and productivity for the business process and systems.

6. The vision and mission statement are important tools for strategic planning. They help to guide and shape the strategy that is well aligned to achieve the desired outcome for the future.

3. Who?

Know Who You Want

Who is Your Target Market?

The first step for your value-adding business is to create or update your business plan. You need to examine and understand your ideal client. Create a picture of the person most likely to purchase your product or service. Is your ideal client a forty-two-year-old female or an established business owner earning over $100,000 in revenue? The first thing I ask entrepreneurs at networking workshops is to tell us their ideal client. This allows the group to know what type of prospective client we should refer to them. If you can paint a picture or avatar of your ideal client, you will have a better idea of how to create your marketing strategy.

The business plan is an exercise to clearly define your product and your target market. You want to define where you will market your product or service. What are the demographics, economic, social, and cultural factors of your ideal client?

You need to be aware of cultural differences if you are marketing a product. For example, when I was going door to door marketing a new financial business, I faced a high percentage of Islamic prospects. A large percentage of Muslims adhere to Sharia law as part of their culture and faith tradition, which means they want no product or service that generates interest income.

If you are selling investment products to a conservative Islamic prospect, you would need to limit your products to energy, gold, or real estate. This is one reason Islamic folks invest in real estate because it doesn't generate interest income, or they can finance through an Islamic loan company. Muslims are very entrepreneurial and would prefer to support brothers of their own faith. You would likely need to be a member in the mosque or have a B2B product or service to sell to that type of target market. Furthermore, Muslim families tend to be more traditional with the wife looking after the children as a homemaker. For Islamic prospects, don't waste your time trying to sell something to the stay-at-home wife while the husband is doing business overseas.

Another type of culture I faced when marketing my financial business was Asian families. Because of the high level of control in communist China, as well as government corruption, there is a lot of distrust from Chinese about doing business. Generally, they have a low risk tolerance and carry very little debt. Many prefer secure investment products such as guaranteed investment certificates or deposit notes. Chinese families are also more traditional and prefer to do business with people who speak Mandarin or Cantonese. However, once you can show value and demonstrate your capabilities, you can build the bridge of trust to allow business to happen.

The more specific you can be in identifying your target market, the more successful you will be. For example, if you run a financial or real estate business to residential families, you may wish to target women. Women are the decision-makers in Western families. Women often make the big decisions that will affect the children; they put more thought into decisions and will contemplate all options before moving ahead with a decision. Women also will ask for referrals from mom groups and friends. If you can obtain a client or customer already in this demographic, it may result in many more leads.

Complete the first Business Plan worksheet. You can use this spreadsheet to write down your vision, mission, ideal client, value proposition, and a clear strategy of how you will market to your ideal client.

See Business Plan Worksheets
Appendix A: Vision, Mission & Ideal Clients

Here are six reasons why you should identify a target market:

1. Allows your business to focus marketing efforts in the most cost-effective way possible. You can understand your consumer's needs through market research.
2. You can craft a specific message to your target market that will appeal to them, including their goals and challenges. If you are an interior designer, your message can be customized to appeal to a high-end homeowner or a senior who is looking to downsize.
3. Focuses on the market that is most likely to purchase your product. By refining your target market, your budget can be directed toward your highest-potential-profit customer.
4. Allows you to reach the right audience of your market plan. By targeting the end user of your product, you

can tailor your message to the person who will purchase your product or service. So, if you are marketing a cleaning or laundry product, you may want to target moms, who are typically doing most of the cleaning or laundry.

5. Allows you to identify the underserved market. You can focus your marketing strategy on a smaller or unreached segment of the total market by defining a niche market. This can be beneficial so that you do not have to compete with larger competitors.

6. Cost-effective strategy for media advertisements. Rather than purchasing ad space in every magazine, you can focus your marketing on those popular with your audience. This way you won't waste money on ad space for those unlikely to purchase your product.

4. What If?
Know Your Business

Strengths, Weaknesses, Opportunities, and Threats (SWOT)

Most people in sales or marketing are familiar with this concept. SWOT stands for Strengths, Weaknesses, Opportunities, and Threats. If you can invest a lot of time and thought into a SWOT analysis before you market and grow your business, it will save you a lot of grief later. To understand SWOT, watch episodes of *Shark Tank* or *Dragons' Den*. The entrepreneurs will come out and pitch the strengths of their business features and benefits. The "dragons" or "sharks" will proceed in pointing out all their weaknesses or confirm their strengths. They will explain the threats that the entrepreneurs may not have considered. A weakness may be that you are competing with a global brand with deep pockets with well-established distribution and marketing.

What Am I Good At? (Strengths)

What makes you different? What makes your business different? If you are a business coach, personal coach, or personal trainer, why would I hire you and not the thousands or even millions of other coaches or trainers out there? Some of the most successful trainers or coaches have created an entire brand and teams around them that follow their school of thought.

Take Beach Body, for example. If you want to become a personal trainer or offer innovative workouts at your new gym, you will be competing against well-established global brands with a proven workout methodology, including Insanity, P90X, and, more recently, Lift. Be thinking about how to use these established brands to your advantage. It could be to promote one of these workouts or aim to eventually sell your fitness plan to one of these established brands. If you take an approach to discredit or criticize one of these established brands, you risk alienating yourself. Better to focus on what makes you different or what new ideas or innovations you bring to the table.

One of the most successful personal trainers I have witnessed was a local fitness trainer who specialized in doing physical training for seniors. She built her clientele by visiting seniors' homes and booking group training sessions. By specializing her business in one target market, she was able to establish a credible brand and build a referral-based business where there was a market need.

What are My Weaknesses?

Pretend you are going on *Shark Tank* or *Dragons' Den*. What are Kevin O'Leary and Mark Cuban going to say after you give your pitch? Usually, the problem is that the entrepreneur has an inflated sense of their business worth compared to the actual earnings. It could also be something more obvious like a bad business idea to begin with. Have you seriously considered the scope and significance of your competition?

Have you put together your five-year plan that outlines how you will scale your production line as your company grows? The first biggest mistake people make is they try to do it all themselves. You must look at yourself in the mirror and identify your greatest strengths and weaknesses. You may be very strong in sales and marketing but hate numbers and administrative work. You may have an accounting background and love numbers but are not comfortable selling your business.

A big mistake an entrepreneur can make when they hire staff is they hire someone who is like-minded. The first person you hire or outsource should be someone with complementary skill sets strong in those areas you are not. If you are weak in crunching numbers or tracking taxes or expenses, work with a bookkeeper or a businessperson with experience in budgeting to help you with your numbers. If you are strong in numbers but hate sales and marketing, partner with someone who knows how to create and influence people; maybe make them a business partner or invite them to be a commissioned salesperson.

I know of a local website designer who understood his weaknesses. He was very good at finding a price point and market for his websites, but he was not very strong at sales. He partnered with a local influencer who was well established on social media and had a network marketing sales background. He gave this salesperson a decent commission so they would both benefit from any resulting new business. By partnering with someone with complementary skill sets, you will set yourself up for success.

Where are the Opportunities?

In 2020, humanity faced a novel COVID-19 pandemic. This resulted in a complete economic shutdown as individuals and businesses were forced to close their doors unless considered an essential service. Investors panicked and sold off equities only to drive the stock market to one of the sharpest declines in history. It was a shock to many business owners because they had no control over the situation. Many felt victimized as they were forced to shut down and terminate staff.

Companies faced some major choices. They could weather the storm until the economy returned to normal in eighteen months. There was a lot of anger and frustration about the social isolation faced in the first few weeks. However, once the government subsidies were paid out, most of the complaining stopped. Individuals and entrepreneurs were forced to look at themselves. This was a time of reflection as families were now spending more time together. If you were not happy in your occupation, this was a time to evaluate your options. Some desired to change from a nonessential business to one considered an essential service.

This forced a lot of businesses to improve their online platform because this was the new reality. You either had to run your business online or you would not have a business. Grocery stores improved home delivery and pick-up options. E-commerce businesses took off as retailers offered more products online and increased social media marketing platforms.

During the Great Depression, many lost jobs and struggled to get by. Many people were depressed and faced hardships to pay for their families. A man named Leo specialized in making amplifiers and lost his job as an accountant twice during the depression. However, he noticed that music and arts were very popular and developed his amplification business. He partnered with a Rickenbacker guitar-maker to start a new business based on his last name, Fender. Fender is now one of the strongest and most popular brands for amplifiers and guitar. The Great Depression created the largest number of millionaires.

There is a great business opportunity for you if you can take advantage of economic or policy change. Can you be disruptive during an economic or technology transition to create a new business opportunity? By doing so, you could position yourself for unlimited success.

You must be nimble enough to pivot your business and take advantage of new opportunities that arise from change. You must evolve your business and produce products and services that are relevant. You must have the courage to stop any business activities not proving fruitful in generating profits or increasing revenue. If you can pivot your business and take advantage of change, you can set yourself up for future abundance!

What Should I Be Worried About? (Threats)

Remember, the fourth reason businesses fail is because of competition. If you fail to identify your competition, you could face a slow death. There is an expression: you keep your friends close and your enemies closer. You should always have your radar up and eyes open to your biggest competitors. Your Judas (future competitor) may be the manager at your store or that person who called you to ask about your business. That is why you should always be grateful and graceful to other people because you don't want to induce greater motivation to a competitor.

You can face competition in two ways. You can take them on at full force and compete with them—try being strategic by maneuvering around them to obtain greater market share or offer a new product or service at a lower price or a premium price point to undermine your competition.

The second way you can face your competition is to welcome and embrace the competition, helping you to grow and improve your business. Any retail store has had to face the Walmart powerhouse when they entered the food and clothing retail market. A national grocer in Canada was smart to prepare for the Walmart Superstore on the horizon before they moved to Canada.

They hired a marketing professor (also my dad) to run a national shopping study to identify the price points of all competitors; then they donated the food and groceries to local food banks. They positioned themselves to compete by offering a lower price discount grocer as an independent or no-frills model. The Weston brand maintained market share against the Walmart goliath while offering higher quality food at a premium price point through Loblaws. Another Canadian grocer, Metro, adopted a similar strategy in acquiring Farm Boy, which offers fresh, high-quality produce, meat, and dairy.

If you do not adapt or change, you can face a slow death or lose substantial market share. A local gym, which I will call Newbie Co., recently opened, and they had to compete against an established local gym, Great Co. The owner of the Newbie gym was originally an instructor at the Great Co. gym. So, he established his own brand, Newbie gym, by focusing on the science of working out. He charged a premium higher price point and had a focused target market that included people with disabilities.

He focused on service by establishing a brand based on personal relationships with his clientele. This gave Newbie gym a family atmosphere, where all the trainers know you by name. By focusing on a specific target market and creating a friendly atmosphere, he was able to compete against a very successful Great Co. gym, which already had celebrity endorsements from NHL hockey players and MMA fighters.

Here are four important strategies on why and how you should complete a SWOT analysis for your business:

1. A SWOT Analysis gives you an unbiased opinion of your business as a whole. It can train your brain to identify every factor or possibility that could affect your business. If the time comes when you are facing a difficult decision or strategy in your business, the SWOT analysis provides essential details to help you develop an action plan based on these key four areas.

2. A SWOT analysis should be a collaborative effort between multiple areas of employment in your company. The founder and owner are the most important, but you can also receive valuable feedback from other staff members who can provide an alternative perspective. This is particularly important for discussing weaknesses. You may be amazed by the creativity and problem-solving suggestions of your team.

3. You can set up a SWOT analysis as a grid and ask yourself relevant questions for each of the four categories. Here are some suggestions for questions you can ask yourself in each section:

   ○ Strengths:
      ■ What do you do well?
      ■ What unique skills or services do you have?
      ■ What can you do better than your competitors?
   ○ Weaknesses:
      ■ What areas of the business can hinder progress?
      ■ What skills are lacking?
      ■ What is costing money?
   ○ Opportunities:
      ■ What can be improved?
      ■ What can you do better for your customer?
      ■ How can you expand your business?

- o Threats:
  - What external elements could damage your performance?
  - What do your competitors do well?
  - What is going on in your industry?

4. Evaluate your results after you complete your SWOT analysis. Look at your strengths to see what can be improved to maintain these strengths. Examine your weaknesses and determine what area of your business they are related to. By identifying the area, whether it is staff, location, or competitors, you can begin to address these weaknesses. Next, determine if there are any time constraints with the opportunities. After that, you can put an action plan together and take advantage of the opportunities. With your SWOT analysis completed, you will have a road map to get you from where you are now to where you want to be in the future.

Take a moment to examine your business and identify your strengths, opportunities, weaknesses, and threats. By doing this exercise and revisiting these aspects, you can obtain clarity on your business.

See Business Plan Worksheets
Appendix B: S.W.O.T. Analysis

5. Be Smart and Scale
Plan Your Business

Be Smart

So, you believe that you have a valuable product that will benefit others. You have a clear vision of what you want to achieve with your business. You have a clear picture of your ideal client, and you have completed the first Business Plan Worksheet. You are now ready to update your business plan. But it is not just about creating or updating a broad business plan with big targets and revenue projections. You need to scale your business by examining where you are today and understanding where you want to get to.

Start by focusing on small, measurable goals to scale your business as you grow. Make sure your goals are SMART. SMART stands for Specific, Measurable, Achievable, Relevant, and Time-specific. Try not to generalize and say: I want to have a six-figure business. But rather, I want my business to have earnings of $105,000 by December 1, 2026. This is very achievable if your business earned $60,000 in 2023, $75,000 in 2024, and $90,000 in 2025.

Here are the specific elements of S.M.A.R.T. for defining your business goals and objectives.

Specific: The aim of this first category is to answer the five Ws of your goal. *What* do you aim to accomplish in your goal? *Why* is this goal important? *Who* will be involved in completing this goal? *Where* is it going to be located? *Which* resources or limitations are there to completing this goal? By answering the five Ws, you will have a clear idea of what the exact specifications are for achieving your objective.

Measurable: The purpose of having a measurable goal is to track your progress and stay motivated. You may have specific objectives you wish to accomplish in your marketing strategy. However, if you are not tracking the results, you will not be aware of the effectiveness of your strategy. By tracking your progress, it will help you stay motivated and focused and have awareness of where you are in completing your deadlines. The three most important *how* questions to ask for measuring the results are: How much? How many? How will it be accomplished?

Achievable: It is important to be realistic in setting a goal. You should base your objectives on what you have achieved in your past so that you know it is attainable. You can stretch your goal by pushing yourself; however, still try to remain realistic and stick to that which is possible in reaching your objective. By setting achievable goals, you may also identify other opportunities or resources that were previously overlooked and get closer to your end result. You should ask yourself: How can I achieve this goal? How realistic is this goal based on the financial budget or other constraints?

Relevant: It is important to evaluate how much your goal matters to you and your business. It is also essential to have support in achieving your objective and to maintain control of your goal. To accomplish this, make sure your goal is moving your business and your team forward. Ultimately it is your responsibility to achieve your goal. Here are some questions you can ask yourself to judge the relevancy of your goal: Is it a worthwhile goal? Is it the right time to achieve this goal? Does it fit with the goals of others? Am I the best person to accomplish this goal?

Time-specific: You should have a target date or deadline for achieving your goal. This can be broken down into both quarterly targets and annual targets. Having a deadline will give you something to work toward and stay focused on. This also helps prevent distractions of everyday tasks by having clarity of your vision and destination. You can break a long-term goal into smaller segments. Ask yourself: When do I want to accomplish this goal? What do I want to achieve in thirty days, sixty days, and ninety days? What do I want to get done this week? What do I want to accomplish today?

See Business Plan Worksheets
Appendix C: S.M.A.R.T. Goals

Scale Your Business

The biggest mistake I made when I launched my promotion company was I hired international talent rather than going local. If you can, try to avoid high-interest debt, because the interest will continue to haunt you for years to come if you cannot pay it back. Smart business owners start small and scale as they grow. You can have a percentage of your revenue budgeted for marketing, so as you grow, you can invest more in attracting customers. You need to walk before you run if you want to reduce risk and grow your business organically.

If you have not pursued an online strategy for your business, maybe it is time to explore additional marketing systems using a social media plan. This may also help you to increase your exposure online and create more clients for your business. If you are not comfortable working online, then you might work with someone with a strong background in social media or a marketing specialist.

Social Media Branding

There are many opportunities to save money when you create and grow your brand. You can create a high-quality logo on Fiverr and create a free Facebook and Instagram business page for your company. You can release videos on YouTube and highlight those same videos on your Facebook and Instagram accounts. You can share educational ideas or inspirational quotes across Facebook, Instagram, and LinkedIn using software such as Hootsuite. There are even opportunities to create free websites. I am not suggesting sacrificing quality. I am recommending that you be smart with your money and grow your promotional expenditures as your business grows. Once your business is generating sales or you have generated financing from other sources, you can develop your e-commerce platforms, social media strategy, and search engine optimization (SEO).

Scaling is so important to the long-term success of any business. You can see many examples from businesses with a jump start from being on *Shark Tank* or *Dragons' Den* only to be undermined by supply issues that damaged their brand. If you are not ready to scale your business, then wait longer until you can fulfill your orders. While it is important to take advantage of opportunity, your brand and reputation will suffer if you are not positioned for success and don't scale properly.

6. How Much?
Know Your Numbers

Understand What Your Business is Worth

So, you have defined your mission, vision statement, and ideal client. You have identified the strengths, weaknesses, opportunities, and threats you will have in your business. Next, you need to understand your current numbers. Once you know where you are at now, then you need to know where you want to be next in one, five, ten, and twenty years. The reason this is important is that you don't want to fall into the number two trap of why businesses fail: they run out of capital because they did not budget properly.

You may also have a goal to sell your business in a specific period of time. If so, you should have a clear idea of who you want to sell to and how much you want to sell for. Then you should be reevaluating this each year with your business plan. You never know when a global pandemic may put a wrinkle in your business plan, so always have a Plan B.

Your business investor pitch will fail if you don't know your numbers. If you are not sure of your numbers, then you need to speak to a bookkeeper or someone with an understanding of numbers to help you figure them out. At the minimum, keep a spreadsheet recording all your income, expenses, and revenue. You need to know if you are losing money, making money, or breaking even. If you are losing money, you should have a goal timeline to when you will become profitable.

You also must be realistic about your business valuations. If your earnings are $10,000 for the year, there is no possibility that your business is worth $1 million. You don't need to spend thousands of dollars to meet with an evaluator. Any accountant or even an experienced bookkeeper should be able to help you prepare a balance sheet and income statement to determine your profitability margins.

Forecasting Business Revenue

Forecasting your business revenue is important so that you can develop your operational and staffing plans to help make your business a success.

Here are three strategies for forecasting your future business revenue:

1. Start with expenses rather than revenue: When you are in the early stages of your business, it is much easier to forecast the expenses than the revenue. You should start by listing the expenses in the most common categories that include the following:
    o Fixed Costs/Overhead: rent, utility bills, phone bills, accounting/bookkeeping, legal/insurance/licensing fees, postage, technology, advertising, and salaries.

(You should triple the legal/licensing fees because they are difficult to predict and usually exceed expectations.)

- Variable Costs: costs of goods sold, i.e., materials, supplies, and packaging.
- Direct Labor Costs: customer service, direct sales, and marketing. (It is a good idea to double your marketing cost projections since they often increase beyond expectations.)
- Direct Sales/Customer Service: It is important to track your direct sales and customer service time as a labor expense so that you can forecast these expenses when you have additional clients.

2. Forecast revenue using both conservative and aggressive scenarios. If you are like most entrepreneurs, you will fluctuate between a conservative reality and successful "dream state" where you will be motivated and inspirational to others. This will allow you to think big but also be realistic to other possible realities.

- Conservative scenario: you should use a low price point, two separate marketing channels, no sales staff, and one new product or service introduced each year over the first three years.
- Aggressive scenario: In addition to a lower price point, you can use a higher price point for a premium product or service, three to four marketing strategies used by yourself and possibly a marketing manager. Account for acquiring two commission salespeople and one product or service introduced in the first year followed by five products or services introduced for each market segment in years two and three. By having ambitious forecasts, you are more likely to

have breakthroughs and innovative ideas to help grow your business.

3. Check the important financial ratios to ensure your projections are sound. After creating aggressive revenue forecasts, it is easy to neglect your expenses. Entrepreneurs are often overly optimistic about reaching revenue goals and assuming expenses will be adjusted to accommodate if the revenue targets are not reached. The best way to reconcile your revenue and expenses is by using a few key ratios to direct your thinking.

    ○   Gross margin: The ratio of your total direct costs to total revenue during a quarter or fiscal year. Be aware of expense margins that increase by 10 or 50 percent. If your sales or customer service expenses are high now, they are also likely to be high in the future.

    ○   Operating profit margin: This is the ratio of your total operating costs (including direct costs and overhead) to total revenue during a quarter or fiscal year. Financing costs should be excluded. This margin should be moving in a positive direction as your revenue increases and your overhead costs represent a lower proportion of your overall costs. The mistake that is often made is entrepreneurs forecast reaching the break-even point earlier and assume they won't require financing.

    ○   Total head count per client: Divide the number of employees at your company by the number of clients you have. This is especially important if you are one person running the show. Do you want to be managing that many accounts in five years after your business has grown? If not, you should revisit your revenue and payroll expenses.

Where Am I Going with My Business?

Building an accurate budget and growth projections will take time. Including your budget and projections in your business plan will help you avoid expenses in the future. If you eventually have a board of directors, they will often expect you to have quarterly updates of your projections. Incorporating aggressive projections can be inspiring as you see what that would do for the bottom line of your company.

Once you have your framework, you can update your business plan. You can work with your accountant or bookkeeper to update your budget. You can review your sales activities to understand what is profitable by examining each sales action and determining the outcome. Every quarter you should be reviewing your sales activities to determine if they are working or if they need to change. If they need to change, update your business plan, and change your sales and marketing activities. Be mindful that it often takes one hundred days to see the results of new sales or marketing initiatives.

See Business Plan Worksheets
Appendix D: Business Numbers

Long-Term Goal

Once you understand your numbers, you can then set out your one-year goal of where you want to be the same time next year. Next you can determine your five-year goal. Your goal may be to increase your revenue by 5 percent, 10 percent, 15 percent, or 20 percent each year.

Also review your personal "Why." What kind of lifestyle will you be able to enjoy once you achieve your desired business income? Will you have enough money to purchase that car you've always desired, complete those kitchen renovations, enjoy that trip down south? Update your vision board and give yourself a daily reminder of what you want to achieve for yourself or your family.

When you align your personal vision of life with your business, you will have the desire and passion to achieve greatness. Once you have the blueprint complete, you are ready to set your plan in motion and chart your course. Without a clear blueprint, your business will not have a proper foundation. It will be like having a poorly built home that may fall apart or droop, end up with cracks in the drywall, or get a leak in the plumbing.

If you have determined your business is worth pursuing, make sure you are moving in the right direction that is in line with your values and your mission of changing people's lives. Survey your customers and ask them how you are doing, what they are happy with, and what they would like to see more of. This can help you to solidify your business mission and focus on making a difference in other people's lives.

Look at the worksheets to help you figure out the basics of where your business is today; then you can figure out your future earning goals for one, five, ten, and even twenty years. If you can increase your business by 10 percent each year, then multiply the number by 1.1 to find the next year's earnings. For 15 percent, multiply by 1.15, and for 20 percent, multiply by 1.2. You may continue until the entire sheet is completed.

See Business Plan Worksheets
Appendix E: 20 Year Revenue Goal

Budget Well

Be smart with your money by not spending on your emotion. If you have ups and downs, or if you tend to be a spend thrift when you are feeling good about yourself, try to be mindful of your budget.

I suffered from a minor form of bipolar disorder, and one of my biggest challenges and regrets was always spending too much when I was feeling in a manic state. Later, while I was feeling depressed, I would feel great remorse or regret from the debt I incurred from purchasing things I didn't really need. I would buy music equipment, clothes, or other things that were not necessary. Over time I have learned to moderate my expenditures.

I have never been in a terrible financial position or bankruptcy, but I certainly carried credit card balances in the thousands. A good rule of thumb is to always be able to pay off your credit card balance by the end of the month. This does not mean transferring your balance to another revolving credit line at a lower interest rate. Some people have managed the art of transferring credit card balances over to 0 percent promotions in consecutive terms. However, if you do not manage your debt well, it will only amplify your problem in the future. Many of us will go through this debt cycle. The important thing is to learn from your errors and improve your budgeting and mindfulness in the future.

PART 2:
YOUR BRAND

7. Who Are You?

Your Brand is Everything

The K-L-T Factor

One of the most important factors of marketing your business is the **K-L-T** factor of your product or service. Is your product or service something that your customers can **know**, **like**, and **trust**? If you cannot achieve all of these three fundamental pillars, you will have difficulty marketing your product or service.

Know: How Will People Know My Business?

Does my customer know me and my business? Do they know my product or service? It comes down to how effective you are at promoting your product or service to your potential customers or prospects. How are you going to bring awareness to your product or service? If I try looking up your company, product, or service on the internet, am I going to find it, and what am I going to see? We all know the expression you only have one chance to make a first impression. When your customer meets you or scrolls through your product/service online, they will have made up their mind within seconds about whether they are interested in your product or service.

How are you planning to let your prospects or potential customers know about you or your product/service? Are you going to buy social media ads or hand out flyers? Are you planning to go door to door or give a speech at a community event? Are you going to promote your product or service through your existing social media following? Are you going to run a social media contest or give out samples at a popular sporting event? You need to have a plan to make people know what you will sell. This is all part of your marketing strategy.

Like: How Will I Make Them Like My Product or Service?

This may sound like a no-brainer, but it is surprising to see how many entrepreneurs do not contemplate the likeability of the product or service they are selling. Do you, your product, or your service have a likeable or inspirational brand? Put yourself in the shoes of your customer. If you came across your product or service being sold by someone else, would you want to buy it?

Entrepreneurs who market themselves on social media are establishing their brand with every post. I see some entrepreneurs sabotaging themselves by posting a rant, a religious or political opinion, or a sexual image that would either offend people or annoy someone. Remember what your father or mother told you: never discuss religion, politics, or sex at the dinner table. Well, the same goes for social media.

If you post something in favor of a conservative or republican, you will irritate a supporter of the liberal or democratic party. If you post a Hindu event with a picture of Ganesh, the elephant-headed Hindu god of beginnings, your potential customers will be left scratching their heads at your exotic spiritual beliefs. Lastly, if you post a flyer of yourself or a scantily clad model, you may receive a lot of likes from men, but you are certainly not going to leave your female friends wanting to introduce your product or service to their husbands. If you are attractive, you can use your assets, but let's keep it classy. The only exception would be if you are marketing a new business venture in the fitness or adult entertainment industry.

It is best to avoid ranting on social media, unless you can laugh at your own foolishness at the same time using self-deprecation. With every passionate opinion, there will always be someone you annoy, whether they say something or not. If you are upset about something, take twenty-four hours until you have a clear head and give yourself some time to reflect before you take any actions you may regret. You don't want to sabotage your own personal brand to your potential customers before you even start. If your social media followers are enjoying your posts and gaining value from your insight, they are more likely to support your business venture because they *like you*!

Trust: Why Should They Believe What I Say?

This is the credibility factor. If you need to ask about health, we automatically trust medical doctors and PhDs because they have spent six to ten years studying and researching that topic. Education or designations is one way to establish credibility. Experience above all goes a long way. It is a lot easier to work and trust someone working in a field for ten years versus a six-month newbie. Through experience, you can obtain client referrals and testimonials that demonstrate your capabilities to other new potential clients.

One reason that we often ask our friends and family for referrals is that we trust their judgment. In my industry of the financial services, it is a lot easier to receive new customers from client referrals than it is to obtain a new client from knocking on their front door. The clients I have obtained by face-to-face door knocking can take three to six months of building trust before they become a client. It is a lot easier to obtain a new client through a warm referral and important to show gratitude when it happens.

If you offer a service, trust is formed by building relationships with your prospective clients. You can achieve this through social media or emails by sharing educational content. You can also let people see a little of your personality. You could post about your personal interests or hobbies with a post of you with your family pet or doing your favorite activity. If people can relate to your content and obtain value from your educational material, they are more inclined to see the benefit of your services.

If you sell a product, people either like it or not. If it is technology, it should be user-friendly and solve a problem or help users be more efficient. Creating a consistent brand that people can trust and benefit from will pay dividends. Companies like Apple, McDonald's, and Toyota all have reliable brands; customers know the quality of the product and the level of service to expect by association with those brands.

A network marketer approached me about buying his product after I had inquired about what he does. His value proposition was reasonable in that his product would save money and benefit a charity. However, he had no business card. Instead, he presented something printed on a flyer. He was new to this business and relied on his associate in prompting him to attend our business networking event.

My impression was that he did not have sufficient credibility to warrant me buying his product. I did not have faith that his product was reliable or that he was competent. His message was not clear, and his communication was further impeded by a thick accent. In my mind, he had not sufficiently established credibility to sell me his product. I did not have confidence in him, even though he represented an international company that could potentially save me money. In my mind, he had not earned my trust to sell me his product.

WII-FM: What's In It For Me?

It is critical that your product or service brand is tuned into the important frequency of WII-FM: What's In It For Me! I will not purchase your product or service unless there is a direct benefit to me. Are you making my life more convenient? Are you going to save me money? Are you going to help me become healthier? Are you going to bring more joy and happiness into my life? Are you going to improve my home or my technology? Are you going to help me grow my business? If nothing benefits me directly, I am not likely to spend my hard-earned money to purchase your product or service.

Many of you have seen *The Wolf of Wall Street* when Leonardo DiCaprio's character playing Jordan Belfort asks his colleagues to sell a pen. The first instinct would be to discuss the features of the pen, such as the color and style. It is not until the one guy asks Jordan to write his name down that the pen becomes an instrument required to solve a need. The ability to position your product or service as a benefit that solves a problem rather than to describe the features is the art of WII-FM.

Working in the financial services, it is easy to get caught up in demonstrating the highest returns for clients or the lowest cost of the management fees. However, once you show that you can help pay for their children's education or help them enjoy greater freedom in retirement or save $250,000 in estate taxes, then you are showing that your services can provide a direct benefit to your potential client.

Put yourself in your customer's shoes and try to view your product, service, or the brand you have created through their eyes. It is valuable to get feedback from other people to make sure you are on the right track. Before you spend your money investing in websites, business cards, manufacturing your product, or developing your services, make sure you have a truly valuable product or service that can indeed benefit people. Make sure it is something that they will want to spend money on.

Ask around and see if your friends will pay money for what you want to sell. Is there a chance you are on the wrong path or direction? Not that your next idea may hit the nail on the head and be the million-dollar bonanza. You just want to make sure you are on the right track before investing the time, money, and energy to create a product or service that can truly benefit others.

Helping Your Client's Decision to Buy

Here are three ways a strong brand increases your customer's buying decision.

1. Time: Customers and clients are often short on time and have to make a fast buying decision. If you have a strong brand, your prospects will be able to make that buying decision with confidence.
2. Trust: By clearly demonstrating what your business stands for, your prospect will have more trust in your brand. Having credibility is imperative in the decision-making process of your prospective client. If you have multiple unrelated product or service offerings,

that can weaken your brand and cause confusion. If you run multiple businesses, it is sometimes best to have separate brands.

3. Choice: There are several related product and service purchase options for your prospective client. A strong brand will clearly demonstrate your value proposition. Once your client sees what makes your brand unique, they will choose to purchase from you over your competitor.

8. Where are You Online?
Improve Your Brand

Can You Improve Your Brand?

Revisit your marketing material, logo, and brand to see if it can be improved. Brand is everything. A real estate investor and public speaker created a strong brand by calling himself the "#1 Business and Wealth Coach." JT Foxx was a millionaire by age twenty-five in real estate and public speaking. Every time he spoke, he introduced himself as the "#1 Business and Wealth Coach." After hearing this enough, you could repeat his branding pitch. The turning point for JT was when he produced a colorful brochure that he would leave at every prospect meeting. He would make sure he was the last person to pitch the real estate opportunity.

Your brand should be unique and reflect the quality and strength of your business to your potential customers and clients. A DIY logo or constantly changing font colors in your marketing material could create anxiety for your potential customers toward your brand. Have a strong logo and image that reflect your vision and mission of your business. If it ain't broke, don't fix it.

Is your brand getting the recognition it deserves? Consider running a marketing promotion in a Facebook or Instagram advertisement or run a giveaway promotion. People love free things. Consider running a drawing in a Facebook ad to help get your brand out there. If you are starting a new social media account for your business, run an incentive by having a drawing for the first fifty "likes."

Google Yourself

People cannot buy a product or service if they don't know about it. Have you tried Googling your business to see what comes up? If you were someone else looking for your service, would you do business with yourself? Are you distracted by other images you see online? Review your SEO, i.e., search engine optimization. If you do not have this in place, it may be time to speak to someone in marketing or a website business to find out how to get your business at the top of the list. You want to improve the search results that direct traffic to your website. That allows people to purchase your product/service or learn more about your business.

Make your brand relevant and current. If you have not adapted your marketing to the new normal in dealing with pandemics and change, then you may be missing the boat. If you can relate to the current situation, you are more likely to be viewed and explored. Companies that pivoted their marketing to the new reality from when the pandemic hit will be more successful in their businesses afterward. Those that kept plodding along with the same old advertisements appeared insensitive and potentially became irrelevant to their highly sensitive and vulnerable customer.

Look at the success of Zoom from March 2020 when COVID-19 spread to North America. The company jumped from $850 million to $1 billion in medium annual revenue. Make a business that people want and need so you can succeed. The mistake that 20 percent of failed businesses make is they create a product or service they love and enjoy but nobody else wants to buy, no one needs, or nobody knows about. Make your product or service relevant so that your business will succeed.

Be Consistent and Keep It Professional

Check your social media presence for consistency and professionalism. Complete a full 360-degree review of your social media platform. Is your brand consistent and clear? Does it look professional? If there are blurred images or unfocused content, then it is time for a marketing makeover. Create a brand that is a magnet for your ideal customer.

Are you utilizing videos to promote your business? If you are not, consider using that as a new strategy to market your product or service. If you are not comfortable making videos, you could consider hiring a voice actor to read the script. Push yourself to be uncomfortable to get results. If you are not comfortable with public speaking, consider joining Toastmasters International to improve the quality and presence of your speech.

Check your video equipment and lighting to make sure your voice is clear and your background is consistent. Ideally, you want to be posting videos each week adding value on a topic related to your business. Consider making your brand more personable by showing a little of your private life and interests.

Some of the most successful influencers are very transparent in their lives. They have created valuable brands by showcasing their personality in their reality shows. Some examples include the *Kardashians, Jersey Shore, Housewives, Million Dollar Listings*, etc.

The more you can put yourself out there, the more valuable you become as a familiar face. This allows potential clients to know, like, and trust you and your business. The music industry understands this branding tool well when they transitioned child actors to singers like Demi Lovato, who starred on *Barney*, or Arianna Grande, who played Cat on Nickelodeon show *Sam and Cat*.

You may also consider creating a click funnel to create familiarity with your brand. A click funnel is a landing website page that includes a link to purchase your product or service. Click funnels typically contain multiple pricing options to purchase what you are selling. For example, options could range from purchasing a book to enrolling in a course or purchasing a high-level coaching program.

You can market your click funnel by creating a Facebook ad with a catchy or provocative caption that leads prospects to your landing page or funnel. This marketing process will allow you to sell more products and services online. The common formula is to offer a free book plus shipping or a relevant tool that leads the prospective client to a low-cost service and then upsells to a premium service. To sign up, your prospect must include an email that will be automatically added to your email list via Mailchimp or similar software. This has become an effective tool that has helped create many multimillionaires in the social media universe world we live in today. You can research successful entrepreneurs in this area, including Russell Brunson or Brendon Borchard.

Online Brand Presence

Here are five ways to build a strong brand presence online:

1. Put in the effort: Having an online brand presence is everything these days and requires an investment of your time and money. Wherever your prospective client contacts you, there needs to be a consistent message across

all mediums. Make the effort to ensure that any customer touchpoint with your product is a positive one.

2. Maintain a good reputation: You and your company should be motivated to get positive reviews and avoid negative reviews at all costs by appeasing your customer. You also need to maintain a positive reputation for your SEO. That may mean having daily or weekly status updates and reviews. You can also monitor sites such as Yelp, AdWords, and Angi. Always try to underpromise and overdeliver for your product or service and leave your new customers with a "wow" experience!

3. Consult with a web designer: You should review the websites of your competitor and consult a professional web designer. Review how your website is trending online. A web designer may give you ideas for how to increase traffic and improve your SEO.

4. Be a good storyteller: To have an effective online presence, you should be able to speak to your audience in a story. This can be achieved through photos, videos, posts, and blogs on mediums such as Facebook, Instagram, YouTube, or LinkedIn. Ensure that every touchpoint your prospective client has tells a compelling story.

5. Start with a strong website: A strong brand starts with a professional-looking website. You should be tracking your analytics to see how your clients are being found. Increase focus on those online strategies that are working and adjust those that are not to discover new opportunities. If you are strong on Facebook or Instagram, you could try exploring other effective mediums such as LinkedIn or Twitter.

PART 3:
YOUR PURPOSE

9. Your Why
What is Your Purpose?

Mindset is Everything

You are what you think you are, you earn what you think you should earn, and you will become what you think you will become. The money you earn right now is exactly what you should be earning right now. You will also earn exactly what you think you will earn in the future. Your current and future state of being is manifested in your head and will be determined by your thoughts, feelings, and desires for your future life. Your mindset is critical to determine your success in life.

Success in life is not predetermined by the environment you are born into. If you want to change or improve your life, you have the power to do so. You can condition your mind to achieve your desired goals in life. It is not sufficient to say you want to succeed. You must believe 100 percent that you will become successful. You must be specific in what you want to accomplish and what you want to earn in life. Once you have specific goals, you can put your thoughts into action to achieve them.

Do you want to have $100,000, $1 million, $10 million, $100 million, $1 billion? You create your life based on your beliefs and desires. If you don't believe and desire wealth, you will not become wealthy. If you don't care about success, you will not achieve it. If you only want to coast through life and just get by, then the universe may drain you of your resources. The universe gives wealth to those who desire it.

Visionary billionaires such as Steve Jobs, Elon Musk, Jeff Bezos, Mark Zuckerberg, and Bill Gates share a strong life purpose in carrying out a vision they created for their business. They have all had challenges in developing their businesses, but they had the resiliency and growth mindset to never give up and carry their vision to its ultimate and unlimited potential.

Your Business "Why"

Simon Sinek clearly explained the importance of "Why" in his book *Start with Why* for any business to be successful. Most marketing strategies are focused on the *what* and *how* of a business. The *what* is the function whereas the *how* is the feature or benefit of the business. The most successful businesses have a strong "Why," which relates to your vision statement. Simon explained this concept in his 2014 Ted Talk entitled *How Great Leaders Inspire Action*. This video is currently the third most popular Ted Talk of all time with over fifty-two million YouTube views.

Sinek illustrates this concept as a golden circle, much like an archery target with three circles. The outside circle is *what*, as in what the business does. This may include the mechanics or operations of the business. The middle circle as *how* refers to the features and benefits of the business. The bull's-eye in the circle is "Why."

"Why" is the vision of your product; it is the element that will inspire your customer to purchase your service based on a higher mission that you have for your business!

Sinek gives the example of the innovation of Apple and its founder Steve Jobs. What makes Apple different is that they start with "Why" in the way they market their company. Apple's "Why" is meant to be disruptive and challenge the status quo through innovation. Products have a beautiful design and are user-friendly. "Apple only happens to make computers," Sinek explained. By starting with "Why," product users are given a strong call to action to purchase Apple products. Without a strong "Why," consumers will not be motivated to purchase your product or service because it just doesn't feel right.

One may also think of Elon Musk as a man with a strong vision. Not only does he make innovative electric cars and trucks but also an ambitious space program. He managed to combine his innovative vision by sending a Tesla car into space, complete with an astronaut mannequin. His innovation inspires Tesla customers and investors along for the exploration and journey of his unique vision. He even created his own cryptocurrency known as Dogecoin.

One of the great Canadian masters of disruption is Bruce Linton, founder of Canopy Growth Corporation. Bruce saw a unique trend in the Canadian Cannabis industry with loosening government restrictions on the use of marijuana. Bruce managed to create a $20 billion company by focusing on how Cannabis is changing people's lives who are suffering from Parkinson's disease or post-traumatic stress disorder (PTSD). Bruce managed to inspire a $5 billion investment by Constellation Brands and an endorsement from Snoop Dogg under the Tweed brand. Sharing the same fate of Steve Jobs, Bruce was eventually terminated by management. The company is now worth $8 billion in market capitalization.

Bruce went on to invest and develop other innovative companies, including Ruckify, which is listed on the TSX Venture Exchange. He states that, as entrepreneurs, "if you know when public policies are going to change, you can make a lot of money." His current interests include mind-altering natural products that have medicinal benefits. What are going to be the rules in five or ten years? Will they be any different? Is there an opportunity to make money by taking advantage of changes in governmental policies?

What is Your Passion?

What are you deeply passionate about? What sets your soul on fire? Happiness for you may be to get married and have a family. It could be to travel and see the world. It could be to seek knowledge, study, or improve yourself through personal development. It may be to create art, make music, learn to play guitar, sing in a choir, or express yourself through dance or performance art. Whatever will bring you happiness, you should proactively search for these things you desire in life. By seeking your passions, you tell the universe to attract them into your life.

Once you have a wide view of the life you want, you need to make specific goals and take actions to achieve it. You can't just say, "I want to be rich and have more free time." You need to be specific. It may be to create a specific business or earn a specific amount of money by a set time. Once you have a specific goal and a vision, you can take the right action to achieve it. Establish daily affirmations and visualization habits to work toward your goal.

If you create a vision without action, you are creating a delusion. Just as you would use a recipe to bake a cake, you will have a predictable outcome. If you want to be happy, you should make other people happy. Make your list for how you want to leave your mark on the planet. You need to specifically figure out what you want in life. Clarity is important because it leads to the power of manifestation. If your "Why" is big enough and you have a desired reason to achieve it, then the *how* will eventually come to you.

If you know what you want and why you want it, then why don't you have it? The reason is that we are creatures of habit based on the way we were raised and conditioned by society. You must map out your path and take the leap to achieve it. You need a burning desire to achieve your abundance goal in life. If you follow your passion and commit your plan into action, the universe will provide you with the abundance you desire.

Stay True to Your Personal "Why"

You can visualize your personal "Why" and create your vision or dream board to achieve your ideal life. As in life, if you have no plan for your business, you risk going off course or being distracted by something else. The distractions you face may not align with your personal values. Stay true to yourself and try not to cut corners.

If you fall off the rails from your desired goal, change the direction of your life to get yourself back on track. If you are losing sleep at night because you are not in alignment with your goals, take time to reexamine your life. Look in the mirror or in your children's eyes to realize if you are on the right course.

One way to attract and manifest the life you want is by creating a vision board. This will allow you to visualize your dreams and desires and reinforce them every day. By achieving your dreams and goals in life, you can achieve the highest vibration in life of love, peace, and gratitude. By creating a visual representation of your personal desires, you invite the universe to manifest your life vision.

You should also consider completing your wheel of life. A wheel of life originated in Buddhism and is an exercise where you rate all aspects of your life, including Business/Career, Finance/

Wealth, Health/Fitness, Social/Friends, Family, Romance/Love, Recreation/Fun, Contribution/Legacy, Personal Growth, Spiritual, and Self-Image. Some or all these categories are included around your wheel. If you rate each on a scale of one to ten, you can see how round your wheel is. If there are large deficiencies in your wheel, your life will have a bumpy ride.

Here are four steps to manifest your dream business:

1. Set clear goals and intentions: you need to be crystal clear on exactly what you want. Set concrete goals and intentions for your business. This can consist of three things:

    o   How much do you want to make in your business each month?

    o   How many clients do you want to work with each month? What are those clients like?

    o   What do you want to feel like in your business?

2. Follow your intuition: your intuition is what knows the best path forward despite what your conscious mind and ego may think. You want to spend time on the things that feel good to you. By doing things that you enjoy, you will be on the path of least resistance. One of the best ways to tap into your intuition is through meditation. Take ten to fifteen minutes each day in a quiet area to center yourself and focus on your breathing. Be open to any guidance that you receive in your thoughts. Make a list of three things that will feel good to accomplish for the day that excites and inspires you.

3. Stay in a high vibration: energy is important to manifesting your goals. You want to keep your energy as high as possible during the day. The easiest way to do this

is by focusing on tasks that you love to do. You may love social media posts, photography, or creating content. Try limiting the tasks that you don't enjoy, such as bookkeeping or sales. For those who love numbers and sales, it could be the exact opposite time blocking.

4. Work on money mindset: if you are not earning the amount of money you desire in your business, it may be because you have some limiting money beliefs. The good news is that this can be improved. You should read the money mindset bible *Think and Grow Rich* by Napoleon Hill. There are other effective mindset books such as *You Were Born Rich* by Bob Proctor, *Rich Dad, Poor Dad* by Robert Kiyosaki, or *The Wealthy Barber* by David Chitlon. If you are currently struggling with debt, read *Debt-Free Forever* by Gail Vaz-Oxlade. These books will help shift how you think about, talk about, and approach money.

10. Your Vision

Creating a Vision Board for Your Personal "Why"

What is a Vision Board?

A vision board is a collection of images and words that inspire you; it is a tangible inspiration for where you are going. Illustrate your goals and dreams as a visual picture. This activates the law of attraction to achieve the greatest dreams you desire. It includes statements with the images as valuable affirmations of your goal. When statements are affirmations of your goal, you will achieve them.

Your objective is to manifest a tangible representation of where you are going in life. The vision board represents your dreams, goals, and ideal life. By representing your goals with pictures and images, you will strengthen your emotions. Your emotions are the vibration energy that activates the law of attraction. Your brain will work tirelessly to achieve what you give your subconscious mind. You are manifesting what you want to become and how you want to feel once you have achieved it. You want to create a vision board that will inspire positive emotions of freedom, confidence, love, and happiness.

Consider images that represent your goals and aspirations in life. You can place around five images (or anywhere from three to ten images) on a board as either a collage or organized in a specific sequence. The board can either be mounted on your wall or a sandwich board that can be placed on your desk or table. Lastly, you can include inspirational words or affirmations related to your images that will inspire you to achieve your desired dreams and goals.

Creating the Vision Board

Set a relaxing atmosphere while creating your vision board. You can use relaxation items such as candles, music, tea, or bubbly. Browse for images that speak to you and represent your true purpose; then place them on your board. Find pictures that represent the experiences, feelings, and possessions you want to attract in your life. Keep the inspiration alive by placing images on the board to achieve this.

You want to include affirmations, including words, quotations, and thoughts that inspire you and represent your true purpose. Use words that uplift you and make you feel good (e.g., love, joy, courage, perseverance). Vision boards are a form of visual creation to design your life. Strive for beauty, simplicity, and clarity by using fewer images. Depict goals and dreams in all areas of your life. You can create multiple vision boards (e.g., one for career and one for your personal life).

Vision Board Dos and Don'ts

Do spend time each morning and evening visualizing, affirming, believing in, and internalizing those goals. Those things you focus on for forty-five minutes before bed will play over in your subconscious mind, repeating throughout the night. Once those images manifest themselves, feel gratitude for how well the law of attraction has worked in your life. Leave the images there as a reminder for what you have achieved in your life. Keep your vision boards as a chronicle for what you have achieved.

Here is what not to do. Don't use black images that don't speak to you or make you have negative emotions. If there is a discovery of fears, stories, or mental obstacles, work through them. Try not to make your vision board too cluttered. You may manifest a cluttered life and attract an overwhelming feeling of stress or chaos into your life.

Visions do not manifest in themselves but your alignment to those visions will do so.

Creating Your Dream Vision Board

There are several supplies that you should acquire to create your vision board. These include cork board, poster board, paper, colored pencils, markers, paint, glue, pins, tape, and scissors. Collect photographs, magazines cut-outs, or printed images from the internet. You can also print family pictures and include them on your vision board.

You can keep it simple by using cork or poster board to mount your images. You may also paint or print the background or wallpaper of your dream vision board. If you are artistic, you may create an acrylic painting that inspires you. I would suggest using an image from nature or your favorite activity. You can print an inspiring image such as a sunset, mountain, beautiful forest, landscape, or the starry night sky. Consider using a silhouette of an inspirational animal with a sunset or ocean background. Ultimately this is your vision board, so you want to use wallpaper on your vision board that will inspire you.

Your painting or wallpaper print may be attached to a 20X24 or 16X20 canvas. You can purchase canvases at Michael's or an art supply store. You can even make your own frame by purchasing a 2X1X8 piece of pine or plywood from Home Depot or your local hardware store. Using a circular saw or miter box with a manual saw, you can cut the wood into four pieces at forty-five-degree angles then use two screws to join the pieces together.

You should create your dream vision board in alignment with either your personal or your business goals. You may even create two vision boards: one for personal and one for business. You may choose specific time periods of one year, five years, and ten (or twenty) years. Collect images and words that represent what you would like to achieve by those specific time frames. This could include a vehicle you want to buy, a home you wish to live in, a person you want to meet, children you want to have, or a vacation you wish to take.

Next, I would choose an image that will make you feel very grounded and happy. This is an image that will comfort you when faced with adversity. For this item, you may choose a picture of your children, spouse, close family member, or best friend. If you are single, you may wish to manifest meeting your future spouse or life partner. Your primary goal will be to become your best true self that will attract this special person into your life.

Lastly, think of the legacy you want to achieve in life. Do you want to create a community, lead a charity, make a positive impact on the environment, or make the world a better place? Find an image that represents your legacy for what you wish to accomplish in life. This could be a picture of family, friends, or a community you wish to give happiness to and provide fulfillment to. For my legacy image, I used a group photo from a charitable fundraising event I hosted for my community that included the mayor, family, friends, and members of the community. The event raised money for a local organization that provides counseling and rehabilitation services for youth struggling with addiction and mental health.

Overall, you should have at least five images for your one-, five-, ten-year (or twenty) goals, your grounding image, and your legacy image. If you are using a painting or wallpaper, I would suggest framing your images with a black border. You can cut out black Bristol board to frame each of the individual images. Cut out the back paper to have a 2 centimeter or ½ inch border on the sides and top surrounding your picture. Leave 6 centimeters or 1 ½ inches for a border below your image for your inspirational word or phrase. You can then select an inspiring affirmation word to include under each picture. You could either cut out a word from a magazine or take a white, silver, or gold marker and write the word directly below the image on the black paper. You are not only creating a dream vision board but also a work of art.

I have completed a vision board as described above. One image included an SUV I was interested in driving and the company had the aim of being one of the safest vehicles on the road. It was a Volvo XC90, which I first discovered in the movie *Gone Girl*, featuring Ben Affleck. I loved this vehicle because it could switch between electric, hybrid, or fully petrol using a special crystal dial. It also had a high-end sound system that was meant to mimic the sound of a Swedish concert hall.

A year and a half after creating the vision board, I was taking my family on vacation to drive from Victoria, BC to Banff, Alberta, Canada. I had originally signed up to rent a full-size vehicle. However, our flight was changed to include a layover in Toronto. As a result, our arrival was delayed two hours and I forgot to advise the car rental company. When we finally arrived to pick up our car, they no longer had any cars left. However, I had an option to upgrade to a van or an SUV, which low and behold, was a Volvo XC90! I was grateful to take my family on our two-week vacation driving a luxury SUV that I had originally manifested on my vision board.

Here are three benefits of creating a vision board:

1. **A vision board creates an emotional connection that motivates you.** This works well if your vision board contains more than just pictures. It should be connected with an emotional experience and a vision.
2. **Your vision board makes your dream real so that you believe it is possible.** The more concrete your vision is in your mind, the more attainable it is. Regardless of how much doubt you may have in yourself, a vision board will help create more confidence and motivation in your belief system.
3. **A vision board clarifies what you want in life because it forces you to put something on paper.** Even if you start with something vague, it can help provide more clarity for your desires once it is written down.

See Business Plan Worksheets
Appendix F: Vision Board

PART 4:
YOUR COMMUNICATION

11. Know Your Customer
Strategic Sales

Four Types of Customers

Most marketing plans paint the target customer with the same brushstroke. There is a generic strategy that aims to target a general demographic, including working-age men and women. This is fine if you run a big corporation with a large marketing budget to cover a large market spectrum. However, if you run a small business and are marketing to individual prospects, you want your communication to be strategic and based on the personality type of your prospective client. You want to aim to have a deeper understanding of that person, so you know how to communicate strategically.

We can break the general population into four main distinct personality types. These four types of people were first identified by the Greek physician Hippocrates. He was the first to explain the four personality types, including sanguine, choleric, melancholic, and phlegmatic. In 1978, Lowry categorized the personality types into true colors of orange, gold, green, and blue where each color represents a different primary personality type. More recently in 2017, Cheri Tree defined these personality types in her book *Why They Buy*. Tree breaks the personality types into four categories, including Blueprint, Action, Nurturing, and Knowledge. By understanding the four personality types, you can use the appropriate marketing strategy and communication to appeal to these individuals.

Initiator: People Person Who Takes Action

The first personality type is known as the Action person by Cheri Tree. Lowry would refer to them as Orange and Hippocrates as Sanguine. This personality type is sociable, enthusiastic, energetic, spontaneous, and fun-loving. They talk more than they listen and are often perceived as being self-assured, innovative, and having a persuasive personality. They prefer a fast-paced environment and may be impulsive. Initiators prefer a stimulating, personal, and friendly environment.

To market to this personality type, use an initiating style of communication. This is a face-to-face, phone call, or virtual interaction that involves socializing, interaction, and sharing stories. You must allow time for socializing at the beginning of your meetings and build rapport by creating a friendly, nonthreatening environment. It is also important to provide time for them to express their feelings and opinion. If you are marketing through a click funnel, you want to be engaging and confident. Tell stories as part of your presentation to build rapport with an action-oriented individual.

Five tips for marketing to an Initiator personality type:

1. **Create a vision**: help them visualize the outcome that they could achieve with your product or service.

2. **Take time to build rapport**: an Initiator wants to feel comfortable in the relationship with you before they do business.

3. **Provide examples of past success**: establish credibility by giving examples of other clients who have achieved success with your product or service. You can also discuss why they came to you, why they purchased your product, and what are the most important features.

4. **Take the role of an advisor**: become the expert to take them through the decision buying process. This can be more effective than overwhelming them with information.

5. **Provide personal guarantees**: Initiators may be risk adverse. By providing the option that they may receive a refund, you can help calm their anxieties that they may experience buyer's remorse.

Direct: Leaders Who Get Down to Business

The second personality type you may come across is the Blueprint personality, according to Cheri Tree. Hippocrates would call it Choleric, and Lowry would call Gold. This is a results-oriented, focused, and competitive person. Personality traits include being quick and decisive as they are motivated to accomplish things. They are independent and confident and prefer a busy, efficient, and structured environment.

You need to use a direct style of communication with this strong personality type. You need to be very clear in your communication as they can be impatient and demanding. Make sure you are punctual for meetings and stick to the agenda. You also want to get right to the point regarding the features and benefits of your product or service. Be very clear in describing the cost, policies, and procedures of your product or service offering.

Five tips for marketing to a Direct personality type:

1. **Be professional**: make sure you come prepared before meeting with a direct personality type. Let them know you will follow up if you don't know the answer rather than give a partly correct answer.
2. **Be efficient**: try not to waste time repeating facts or building your point. It is most effective to cut to the chase and give short and concise answers.
3. **Emphasize how you solve their problems**: it is important to show how your service or product will be useful to them or their organization.
4. **Emphasize the competitive edge**: as they are competitive types, demonstrate how your product or service will help them better against the competition.
5. **Avoid personal opinions or testimonials**: focus on the return on equity that a successful customer had rather than how much they loved your product or service.

Supportive: Warm and Fuzzy People

The next communication style is the supportive communicator. This personality type is a nurturing person, according to Tree. Hippocrates called it Phlegmatic, and Lowry described them as Blue. This communicator is patient, cooperative, and sympathetic. They are an active listener and anticipate the needs of others.

Use a calm and steady style of communication and create a personal and relaxed environment for your meetings. Since supportive communicators dislike change, they may appear to be indecisive. If you are working with a supportive communicator, encourage them to ask for more details or information to make a buying decision. You may also try to give them more details about your product or service in advance so that they will be more comfortable when they meet you in person or virtually.

Four tips for marketing to a Supportive personality type:

1. **Provide case studies**: Supportive personalities want to know that you have their best interests in mind. Give stories of how your business impacted people's lives to demonstrate your track record.
2. **Emphasize the ongoing relationships**: if you have a high level of customer service or long-term partnerships, make sure this receives emphasis.
3. **Less focus on facts and figures**: Supportive personalities make their buying decision on how their business is affected on a human level rather than data.
4. **Summarize as you go**: it is important to get their buy-in, so ask questions along the way such as: "So, we agree that we can further automate your sales process?"

Analytical Communicator: Detail-Oriented

The Analytical communicator loves detail. Hippocrates called them melancholic, Lowry called them Green, and Tree called them Knowledge personality. Analytical communicators are cautious, precise, and disciplined. They are deliberate, methodical, and a problem-solver. They are often careful and diplomatic in their interactions. They strive for perfection within themselves and their surroundings, which often leads to tidy and detailed-oriented behavior.

Analytical communicators value learning, intelligence, and being logical. They are generally skilled in research, development, and technology. They are interested in science, universal truths, and the big picture. When communicating your product or service with an analytical communicator, provide both qualitative and quantitative details. Include bar graphs and tables to illustrate concepts. You want to be thorough and detailed in reviewing the product or service features.

Five tips for marketing to the Analytical personality type:

1. **Don't rush the sales process**: be prepared for a longer selling process as Analytics like to gather all the necessary facts and figures before making a buying decision.
2. **Assume they have done their research**: spend more time discussing personalized and custom solutions for their business rather than the basics. However, do not skip over the introductory material.
3. **Avoid high-level claims**: provide date for any claim made in order to not lose credibility. Analytics may become suspicious if you overhype your product or service in that you may be covering up flaws.
4. **Provide detailed information**: avoid overgeneralizations for the past successes of your business. Better to use hard facts such as "our product increased our client's revenue by 15 percent in year-over-year growth."
5. **Don't force a relationship**: Analytics may become annoyed by those who are overflattering if the feeling is not genuine.

Appealing to All Four Personalities

Understand the personality type of your customer so you can understand the best marketing strategy that will allow them to be comfortable in making a buying decision. If you are running through bars and graphs with someone who values closeness and relationships, you may miss the mark. If you are excited and talking high level to someone who prefers numbers and details, you will have a harder time selling your product. Most people sell based on their own personality type rather than that of the buyer. If you are giving a sales presentation, try to include elements that will appeal to all four different personality types.

In order to appeal to Initiator or action-oriented individuals, you want to make sure you are confident and have lots of energy in your presentation. You want to engage the participants in conversation or breakout rooms if possible. Action-oriented people value the social aspect of the sales process and would be suitable to invite for lunch or coffee meeting.

Direct people prefer to circumvent all the social chitchat and get down to business. If your sales presentation is unprepared or you have a vague presentation, you will lose the Direct communicator. Have a clear strategy prepared with all your points lined up ahead of time. Try to keep things brief and to the point. When you ask for the business, be clear on the price and policies surrounding the offer.

Supportive prospects will appreciate any socially responsible affiliations with you or your company that result in positive environmental or social change. You may need a longer sales process for a nurturing personality type to feel comfortable and secure in doing business with you. You may need to show greater patience and allow them to share their story. They may want to share their values with you or tell you about the hardships that they have endured to build a connection.

Analytical people will appreciate specific information about your product or service. Be prepared to explain your offering with a high level of detail to an analytical communicator. You will need to support your statements with numbers and validity. Have a clear price, payment plan, and return policy. Give quantitative and qualitative examples of how your product or service has solved problems for other customers.

You can attempt to market your presentation to all four personality types. I have seen this managed well in a PowerPoint presentation by JT Foxx. First, he gave a confident talk, which included high-level, valuable educational tips. Next, he gave a clear, step-by-step, effective presentation. He mentioned some of the charitable work he's done in Africa, which would appeal to the nurturing types. Lastly, he gave three clear purchasing options and included a purchase link in the direct message box. By including elements that attract all four personality types, you increase your sales opportunities.

12. What Do You Do and Why Should I Care?
Build Relationships

One-Minute Presentation (OMP)

As a sole entrepreneur starting to market your own business, you should be able to demonstrate your value proposition in a short and concise manner. At this point, you should have the information you need to create your one-minute presentation (OMP.). This is an opportunity to practice conveying your value proposition in a short period of time. You want to provide the most important details and focus on the benefits of your product or service to your target market, not just the features. The "Why" of your business vision is also important to convey to your prospective client.

As I mentioned earlier, the classic example of feature versus benefit is illustrated in the scene in *The Wolf on Wall Street* when Jordan Belford (played by Leonardo DiCaprio) asks his friends to sell him a pen. The other salesmen discusses the features of the pen until finally his friend, Brad, says, "Write down your name on this napkin," and Jordan replies, "I don't have one." Brad then replies, "There you go, supply and demand." The pen may have lovely features, such as a stylus or a brass clip; however, the benefit of the pen is that you can write something. This example teaches you to focus on the benefit you provide in solving a particular problem rather than the features of your product or service.

Creating your OMP will prepare you for a situation when you are in a line at Starbucks or meet an important person in an elevator who is your ideal client. You only have a short period of time to pitch your product. You want to be very strategic in tuning into the WII-FM of your prospective client and not just use the same brushstroke for everyone.

OMP Burger

One way to think of the one-minute presentation looks like putting a burger together. The first step is to describe the meat of your burger. This describes *what* problem you solve. It is the unique value proposition of your product or service.

Here are a couple examples of describing the core value and benefit you provide, which is the meat of your product/service:

- "I help busy people stay healthy using a unique, high-impact fitness plan and wholesome diet to help them lose weight and lead a healthy and happier lifestyle."
- "I provide guidance to individuals who are shopping for their dream home and provide clear strategies for negotiating price in a competitive environment."

The bottom bun is the "Why" to describe the problem that you are solving with your business. You can start with the opening "you know how," "you sometimes find that," "often is the case that," "in today's day and age," etc. Here are some examples:

- "You know how most exercise routines are repetitive, boring, and don't include anything about diet?" (fitness trainer)
- "In today's day and age, it is difficult to buy a home in the current heated real estate market." (realtor)

The top bun is the *how* to explain your methodology unique to your value proposition. Here are a couple of examples:

- "I use a proven exercise regimen using weights, circuit training, and cardio that varies from week to week in order to keep a fresh, new routine."
- "My real estate firm has contracts with top builders in the city and we give our clients first choice to these exclusive listings." or "For each of my clients, I complete a market analysis of surrounding properties, and I educate my clients about the ideal features to look for in their dream home."

Lastly, you don't want to forget your pickle on your burger. The pickle is to provide your tag line. To build your brand and make people remember you and your business, you want to end with a catchphrase or motto for your business to make yourself memorable. This is a time to revisit your three intrinsic value words to help you come up with something unique. A common strategy to use at networking events is to state your name, your business, and your catchphrase to finish.

I would say, "My name is Paul Arnold, Business Strategist and Wealth Coach, *Own Your Truth, Live your Dream*."

Some common corporate catchphrases you may be familiar with are "*Just Do It*" (Nike), "*Don't leave home without it*" (American Express), "*A diamond is forever*" (De Beers), "*Finger Lickin' good*" (KFC), and "*I'm Lovin' it*" (McDonald's).

For individual entrepreneurs, you can use catchphrases like *we care, for remarkable results, your favorite* _____, *best in* _____, *making your dreams come true, making sense of* _____. Extra points if you can relate your slogan to the name of your business in a pun or word play. An example is an Ottawa realtor Mark Granada. He would say, "Your favorite Realtor for Re-**Mark**able results."

Here are eight tips to delivering an effective One-Minute Presentation:

1. **Keep it brief**: your OMP should be between thirty and sixty seconds and a short recap of the *what, how,* and "Why" of your business with a memorable statement.

2. **Be persuasive**: make sure your pitch is compelling by having a strong "Why" for your business. You want to spark your listener's interest in your idea, organization, and background.

3. **Share your skills**: make sure to include your skills to add credibility to your pitch. Without boasting or bragging, you want to demonstrate the unique skills you bring to the table.

4. **Practice**: to have an effective presentation, you should practice until your pitch and speed sounds natural. The more you practice, the easier it will be to deliver at your next networking event or interview.

5. **Keep positive and flexible**: you want to appear approachable, so make sure not to lead with things

about your business that you do not enjoy. You want to make a great first impression with positive enthusiasm.

6. **Have a call to action**: without being too specific, you want to have a desired outcome of your presentation. You need to remember what you are looking for.

7. **Know your audience**: your presentation will be more impactful if you can target your language and communication style to your listener. This may include using industry jargon of your prospect's company and impressing the listener with your knowledge and credibility.

8. **Have your business card ready**: make sure you have your business card ready to hand out at the end as a way of continuing the conversation. Alternatively, you can exchange contact information with your smartphone. You could register for a QR code for your prospect to scan and receive a link to your website. Social media contacts can be exchanged using LinkedIn, Facebook, or Instagram.

See Business Plan Worksheets
Appendix G: One Minute Presentation Burger

Five Cs to Building Relationships

There are the five Cs to build relationships to establish rapport. You not only want to communicate the essence of your business in solving a problem but you also need to build rapport and trust with your ideal prospective client by using some specific relationship-building techniques. Business success is about relationships. You need to network with other professionals and add value.

Let's look at some basic techniques to establish and build a new relationship with a stranger. Imagine yourself having your first coffee meeting or phone call with your prospective client. You may only have twenty to thirty minutes to build trust with this person. Here are some simple physical and psychological communication skills you can employ to build a stronger connection with this person. To make them easy to remember, they all start with the letter 'C.'

The five Cs to build relationships and establish rapport are as follows.

1. Common Ground

Try to find common ground by finding similar interests or experiences with your prospective client to build trust. Maybe you grew up in the same town or both play tennis. Maybe you are both musicians, love baseball, or enjoy crafts. As soon as you can find some common ground, it serves as an emotional bridge that can help engage your prospect. If you both have children, that is an easy way to find common ground by sharing some relatable stories of your kids.

2. Conversation That is Mindful

You can also employ some psychological techniques that will unconsciously make your prospect feel at ease. One strategy is to incorporate imitation in your conversation. That could include mimicking the speaking volume, posture, and tone of your prospect to create a natural bond at a subconscious level. If you prospect speaks in a quiet, reserved tone, you can speak in a similar soft voice, whereas if your prospect speaks loud and fast, you could do the same. If your customer leans forward, you should do the same.

3. Candid Humor

Another great way to establish trust is by using humor to make yourself more likeable.

If you can make your prospect laugh with you, there is a higher chance that they will like you and want to do business with you.

You must be good at reading people to understand what type of humor will be suitable. If they are acting friendly, some gentle ribbing can often be flattering, making your prospect feel like you have been friends for a long time.

If you are in line at Starbucks, maybe there is something funny going on behind the counter you could make a funny comment about. Using self-depreciation humor is the safest way to use humor. You can make fun of your receding hairline, muffin top, or some lazy or odd habits you have. Humor can help provide brevity and build trust. If you are humble and can laugh at yourself, you are demonstrating that you don't take yourself too seriously and are easy to work with. On the flip side, if you are dealing with someone in a suit who looks stressed, humor can sometimes provide a welcome distraction to life.

I recall a Facebook Live presentation I was on. The presenter mentioned she grew up on the East Coast. I put a comment asking if she misses lobster and mussels. She joked by calling me a jerk for reminding her of how much she misses eating mussels. I immediately liked her for her candor and gentle, friendly ribbing.

4. Care
Aim to have your prospect do most of the speaking and demonstrate genuine interest. If you can get your prospective client chatting away, you are going in the right direction. You need only to ask them some questions about their life. If they are only giving you yes or no answers, then that may be a hint it is time to move on.

5. Compliment
Lastly, there's nothing like a few sincere compliments to help build that bond with your prospective client. You could congratulate them about the success they have achieved in their business. Maybe

they have a new phone or gadget you can demonstrate your intrigue for. Make sure your comments are genuine and not "sleazy" like you are trying to ask them out on a date. Some examples of compliments are: "I really like that necklace you are wearing," "What is the meaning of your pendant?" or "I like the pattern on your socks, that Q*Bert game takes me back to my childhood," "Cool tattoos, what do they mean?"

PART 5:
YOUR PEOPLE

13. Dream Team
Build Your Team

Create Your Dream Team

Why is your team important? Remember, the number three reason businesses fail is that they don't have the right team. By building the right team, you can delegate tasks to people better at doing certain things then you are who also provide great ideas to improve your business.

One of the greatest challenges successful business owners face is time management. Once your business takes off, it becomes more difficult to manage all the sales, admin, marketing, and accounting.

When you went off to high school or college, you had a timetable laid out on your calendar. You were able to choose your courses and plan your year. Your classes, group projects, presentations, and exams were all laid out on a well-organized schedule. A well-planned business will have all the moving parts working together as one team. You have the HR, engineers, sales, marketing, accounting, and administration. As a new business owner, often you must wear many hats, but eventually, you can delegate these tasks to others. A good start to optimize your processes would be to consider hiring a virtual assistant.

Think of your company like you are a bank. You have a bank manager, customer service, and financial sales agents. You are part of the executive management team that provides the overall direction of the business. Then you have the regional managers carrying out your vision to your team. The core of the business generating activities is done by your sales team. You may have contract commission sales agents or use Facebook, Instagram, or Google ads to drive your sales. You should have time allocated and roles assigned for all aspects of your business.

Teamwork Makes the Dream Work

Imagine your business as a soccer team. Your strikers are your offence, your marketing are your halfbacks, and your bookkeepers and accountant are your defense to keep compliance and taxes aligned. Your business plan is your goalie, who is responsible for keeping everyone in check. The goalie checks that the team is ready before launching the ball into play. You are the coach leading the team to the next victory. You are trying to score as many goals as possible, but you can only do that through great teamwork.

If you don't keep proper books, you may run into unexpected trouble with the tax department. If your brand isn't polished with a supporting marketing strategy, your customers may lose faith in your brand as you become weathered or out-of-date.

Keeping your team playing well and working together efficiently will help your business run smoothly. You will win more games if you reward great efforts and outcomes. A local entrepreneur, Steve Cody, has a very strong small business track record; he started several successful businesses now totaling over $750 million in sales. The strategy for his last company, Ruckify, was to first hire generalists who could multitask and eventually create more specialized roles in technology, sales, and marketing. Steve emphasized the fact that by hiring the right people, it makes your job easier, and you can spend more time doing what you love.

His former partner, Bruce Linton, created an $8 billion marijuana company, Canopy Growth Corporation. His success came because he rewarded team effort and hard work through issuing company ownership and stock option shares to employees who made a significant contribution. Bruce was focused on rewarding results, even paying select staff more than himself in some instances.

Spend Time on the Right Activities

It is best to start off with one-hour time blocks throughout your day. If you are your main sales driver, 60 percent of your day should be on sales or marketing activities, whether direct sales or communicating with your sales team, 20 percent of your time should be on branding and marketing activities, and 20 percent of your time for personal development and research to see how you can improve your business.

Time-blocking your calendar allows you to maximize your efficiency throughout the day. First, input the most important sales activities early in your day so you can contact people when you are feeling fresh and rejuvenated. The time between 9 and 11 a.m. and 1 and 3 p.m. are some of the better times to call people during the day. Statistically, Wednesday at 4 p.m. is the best time to reach people because they are bored at work and looking for something else to do before they head home.

If you are contacting people working nine-to-five jobs, a 4–6 pm or 5–7 pm call block may work better. You can send messages, make phone calls, schedule virtual meetings on Zoom, Teams, or

WebEx, or meet face to face for coffee. Have time blocks set aside to schedule your client meetings and sales calls.

I like to schedule a Monday morning call to touch base with my team to plan out the week. You can also have a regular morning fifteen- to twenty-minute meeting with your admin, so everyone is on the same page. There are software tools like Basecamp, Zoho, or Asana you can use to organize projects or events with your team. Your team can update the tasks and mark them complete once they are finished. Zoho also has a survey function that allows you to survey your staff and your customers and view the analytics in a visual graph.

14. Right Surroundings
Improve Your Network

Spend Time with the Right People

You are like the five people you spend the most time with. If you want to improve your business and make more money, why not hang out with people who are already achieving that? Take networking, for example. Your typical networking group will have a financial advisor, a realtor, and a mortgage broker. You should also have a lawyer or accountant in your group. The remainder of your group will be direct sales or network marketing entrepreneurs of various stages. Often networking groups attract people who are launching businesses and looking to meet new people.

One of my mentors called these poor people networking groups. If your business is established and you are no longer receiving referrals, it may be time to change who you hang out with. Why not raise the bar of your networking by joining a chamber of commerce or similar business club, rotary club, or Kiwanis? These organizations may have more established business owners who will have a greater benefit to your business.

Why not create or join a mastermind group that has a purpose and motivates you? Napoleon Hill discussed the value of mastermind groups to take your business development to a higher level using the power of thought, visualization, and affirmations. Through a mastermind, you can obtain feedback from other professionals and business owners on how you can improve your business.

Try to find a business coach or accountability partner. If you have no one to keep you and your business accountable, then you will likely stay just as you are and remain stagnant. Find someone or a small group of passionate business owners who will help you grow. Find people motivated and positive who are also hungry to grow their business.

Why not invest your time with those who want to get better? Find a millionaire mentor who has already achieved success in their business and is living a comfortable life. You may need to pay for a coaching session or workshop to get your foot in the door. If the four or five people you hang out with are millionaire business owners, guess what? You and your business will likely become one. If you can find value to bring to others, the rule of reciprocity will apply. Business owners who achieve success are often happy to help others succeed by becoming a mentor. This gives them satisfaction and fulfillment in their lives as a way they can give back.

Choose Your Mentors Wisely

Choose your mentors wisely; evaluate the alignment of their skills with what you need to improve on to achieve greater success in your business. Find a coach in a similar or related field as where you want to improve your abilities. Some established business coaches are seasoned salesman and will only see you as a dollar sign. They will try to capitalize on as much money as you are willing to give them. They are happy to accept your credit card charges and are not concerned about your credit card balance. They will even encourage this by saying "the best investment is the investment in yourself" and give examples of when they maxed their own credit cards to achieve their own success.

You need to understand that they are capitalists, and as the word implies, they are trying to capitalize on the revenue that they can generate from their sales and marketing offer. They will have a good hook and a compelling rags-to-riches success story. They will paint a picture of success, a vision of what you could achieve through their program followed by the irresistible offer. Then they will tag on the risk-reversal, money-back guarantee. This is the exact sales formula that Dean Grazioso and Tony Robbins teach in their seminars. They are great people with great value and are great salesmen. They understand the psychology of sales and are very effective at acquiring new business.

You also need to understand that they may have invested thousands, tens of thousands, or even hundreds of thousands of dollars to create this event or webinar that you attended. Of course, they are looking to recoup their expenses and make a profit because money only comes from one place, and that is other people's pockets.

Occasionally I come across business owners who are still bitter to this day because they felt ripped off or victimized by an established business coach who sold them a coaching program at a hefty price. Try not to make decisions based on emotion or excitement. Sometimes it is best to wait twenty-four hours to decide if a program will truly further your results and give you the opportunities you need to become successful. You are doing a disservice to yourself by holding on to this frustration or anger. Accept it as a lesson to make better decisions in the future.

Get Rid of the Wrong People

It is time to eliminate the negative people from your life. Think of a traffic light and divide your networking into green, yellow, and red. *Green* people are those who are motivated, successful, and hungry to grow. These are the people who are active in networking in person or on social media. They are supportive and motivating to you and your business by "liking" your posts. These people are rare gems who you need to treasure and show your appreciation for!

The *yellow* people are the neutral ones. They are nonresponsive to you and your business. Mostly, they talk about themselves or their interests. The only time they respond is when it is something that will benefit them or have relevance to their life. They will not harm you but also not benefit you unless you reach out to them or present them something they like.

Lastly, we have the *red* people of your network. These people are negative and complain a lot. It is time to eliminate the negative people in your life because they are killing your inspiration. I would suggest cropping up to 25 percent of your Facebook followers if they are people who are not positive in your life. You need to cleanse your business by removing the toxic people. Sometimes this may also be to fire a client. If you find they complain a lot, maybe it is time to refer them to someone else or tell them you can no longer help them. Protect your mental health by raising the bar of the people you allow into your life.

The best way to build your business is to take on clients who you would like to be friends with. If you are dreading your meetings or feeling completely drained every time you meet with a client, develop a new process to keep meetings shorter and efficient. If you have an uneasy feeling or don't feel you are a good fit for a long-term business relationship, sometimes it is better to cut your losses from the start in order to avoid future grief.

It is important to be empathetic to other people and this is something we have learned over the global pandemic of 2020 and 2021. You never know what people are going through. Just because they are ignoring you or unresponsive doesn't mean they don't care. Maybe they are going through a tough time, a divorce, a job loss, or a health crisis. We must be able to put ourselves in other people's shoes and reach out to them when they need our help. If you give of yourself to others, you will also feel better by sharing yourself. Your heart will be lighter, and you will enjoy a more meaningful life.

PART 6:
YOUR PIVOT

15. Change Direction
Six Steps to Pivot and Remain Profitable

Getting Fired from My Commission Sales Business

Back in March 2021, we were impacted by the significant global health pandemic of COVID-19. The hospitality, travel, and restaurant industry were completely shut down. Many lost their jobs and had to rely on government subsidies. Many struggled as we figured out the new work-from-home reality and battled against the invisible enemy. On top of that, we had to deal with social upheaval, including Black Lives Matter, #MeToo movement, and political upheaval and strife of the white house raid. We had to get used to wearing masks, social distancing, virtual learning, and travel restrictions that prevented visiting family.

My life changed when after five months I was laid off from a sales business that I had put my blood, sweat, and tears into building up. I built a six-figure business by knocking on doors, cold calling, and investing in seminars. I had won sales awards and reward trips for my family to beautiful destinations. I had one of the largest offices in my city with over fifteen hundred square feet and a full-time office administrator.

All that came to a halt one day late that summer. COVID-19 had impacted my outreach, and I was not obtaining enough new clients from the virtual webinars I was hosting. After I fell short of my quarterly sales target, I received a call one Thursday morning before work saying I was terminated. I was informed of my severance pay and told not to travel to work that morning as I was being replaced. I thought of my new assistant I had hired five months ago and what she was going to think. I thought of what I was going to do and how I was going to tell my family. My wife sensed something was wrong after I sat in the bedroom for fifteen minutes. I told her the news and she told me that I will figure it out. Well, you know what, I did!

After the shock had worn down, I started taking the necessary steps for my unexpected transition. I booked a time with my replacement to collect my belongings. I rented a U-Haul and had to take my daughters to my former office and load up all the chairs, books, and equipment I had purchased for the office. Then began the long road of figuring out what to do next.

After setting up my government subsidy, I started reflecting on what I would like to do with the rest of my life. I contemplated joining the military, but I was not sure how it would go being in my mid-forties and doing basic training with those twenty years younger. I inquired, but it turned out the military was also set back from the pandemic; they were not hiring as training and applications were getting delayed. In addition, the military life is a young man's game.

But I knew what I was most fascinated with; I wanted to continue the journey of discovery on how businesses can adapt and change while remaining profitable. Back in April of that year, some fellow business owners and myself had arranged an e-conference to share some best practices and stories of business survival. We called it "Adapt & Overcome." I was fascinated by this topic as it reminded me of the Great Depression when so many successful entrepreneurs became millionaires.

I decided to get certified in business analysis and agile methodology. I was fascinated with business strategy and how to successfully pivot and transition a business through a change strategy to become more profitable while minimizing risk. What I would like to share with you next is how most successful Fortune 500 companies successfully deal with change and evolution—the six steps they use to stay profitable and maneuver in a new direction while minimizing risk. If you need help executing the following steps, consider consulting a certified business analyst who is trained on these knowledge areas to oversee change strategy execution. I have adapted these strategies for small business.

Step One: Plan the Framework for Execution

Start by planning your plan. The first thing you need to do is create the framework for executing your business pivot. How are you going to figure out your business needs and objectives? Are you going to survey your customers, analyze your competition, or discover new trends in the market?

The most important thing is to understand the "Why" of your change and the key players in your business who are going to help drive the change. Key players include you, your investors, and most importantly, your customers. Key players could also include your vendors, your tech support people, or your subject matter experts. If you are in financial services, law, or healthcare, you also need to understand compliance and regulation. If you ignore these key players in your business, you will doom yourself to fail before you even begin.

I have witnessed some marketing companies that target financial advisors completely ignore the compliance and regulation in communication to the public. If you want to work in a highly regulated field, you need to understand what you can and cannot say and do, so you do not end up dead in the water. By understanding compliance, you will put yourself ahead of the competition.

Next you need to understand how the decisions are going to be made in your pivot strategy. Who are the most important leaders and decision-makers for this change? Are you going to involve your investors or your accountant? Do you have a business coach to help you evaluate the next critical steps? There will come a time when you need to choose to either turn right or turn left; take the blue pill or the red pill. Most important, as Tony Robbins says: **make a decision**. Whether you get it right or wrong, at least you are moving forward, and if you get it wrong, you can learn from your mistakes.

Lastly, you should find a way to track your findings from your pivot strategy to make sure you are making the right moves. Consider sending out regular surveys to your customers or investors. You can track the analytics of what the key players are looking for from your business. At the end of the day, you are the leader driving your business. However, if you can get some important confirmation and justification for your change strategy, you will be better off. For our business venture, in God we trust, and for everything else, examine the data!

Step Two: Outreach and Collaboration with Key Players

The biggest mistake we make as entrepreneurs is to forge ahead with a new idea before testing its validity. Is your next step a smart idea or is it a misinformed delusion? To find out, we need to reach out to the key players or stakeholders in our business. We want to hear from our customers and investors to make sure we are doing it right. To do this we need to figure out who the key players are and how we are going to reach out to them.

Are you going to send people surveys and use Excel, Survey Monkey, or Zoho to track the results? Are you going to call or direct message the key players and ask their advice? Can you have an informed conversation and bounce your ideas off them? Maybe they will have some suggestions for you. Can you organize a brainstorming session with your business coach or mentor? Whatever it is, get moving and shaking!

Make a list of all your key players or anyone who has "skin in the game" with your business. Determine how you are going to generate feedback from them. If you have investors, you should have regular touchpoints because they have an important stake in your business. Make sure you have a system to track all your results. For your interviews with key players, take notes and record the conversations so that you can store all the important feedback you receive. Taking these important steps will prevent you from heading off track and wasting time, energy, and money on something that will not even produce results.

Once you have figured out who your key players are and how you are going to collect feedback, you need to execute. Send out your surveys, schedule your interviews or brainstorming sessions, and message your key players. Collect your results and store them on a spreadsheet or graph so that you can examine this important data you have collected. What are your findings and how have they either confirmed or contradicted your business strategy? If the results are in alignment with your strategies, then you have justification for your pivot. Consider yourself knighted and ready to carry out your business mission!

Step Three: Key Elements and Strategy Matrix

Are you one of those entrepreneurs who wants to try twenty different strategies to take your business to the next level, such as Facebook, Instagram, YouTube, and LinkedIn social media marketing amongst other things? You need to find a way to prioritize your strategies to grow your business.

It is important to evaluate the key elements of your business change strategy. You need to map out your strategy and track the important key drivers for your business. Are you going to focus on one area of marketing and sales? Are you going to develop a new software platform? You can map out these key elements and prioritize them with the various stages of your business evolution. Consider creating a mind map or diagram to write out all possible marketing and sales strategies for your business.

What do I mean by key elements? Key elements are your priorities for your business change. This could include a cost-benefit analysis of your marketing and sales strategy. This is important for evaluating the benefits of any large expenditures you have.

Examine the risks: if you invest in one strategy for your business, are you going to get the results you are looking for? What are the dependencies in your business; who is going to be affected by your business pivot? Will this change affect existing key vendor relationships that you are depending upon? Is there a possibility of losing any of your partners because they do not support your change strategy?

In addition to cost-benefit and risk, you will need to examine the impact of change relative to your new strategy. You need to consider your priorities by looking at time to market. That which will have the greatest impact is what you should make most urgent. Do you need to bring your product or service to market before your competitor or will you lose market share by delaying six months? Will this change cause instability in your business by affecting your relationships to your staff? Will they be open to change, or will this change make them uncomfortable?

It is important to map out all the change strategies you want to implement. But first you need to prioritize them. The first thing you can do is create a **strategy matrix**, a 2X2 matrix with four squares. On the vertical or axis, you have least profitable to most profitable. These are the financial results if successfully implemented. On the horizontal axis, you should have beginner to expert. This contrasts strategies you do not have experience in versus strategies you know you will excel at.

Say, for example, you have worked in a profession and now want to become a coach in your related field. Create your strategy matrix. You may be experienced at public speaking since you are always giving PowerPoint presentations at work. But maybe you do not have experience with website design. Maybe you are comfortable at social media marketing but not so good at sales. You can map out all the areas in which you are a beginner and in which you are expert. Then you can determine what strategies are going to be most profitable. If you have a lot of strategies to input, you could make it a 3X3 matrix and include intermediate and somewhat profitable as the middle squares.

If you create a funnel and Facebook ads, will that be more profitable than if you go on public speaking tours where you are a subject matter expert? Do you write a book or sell online courses? What will have the greatest economic benefit, and what do you excel at? These are things to discuss with an experienced mentor or business coach to help you evaluate the potential results.

What you are an expert at and what is most profitable for your business will be the strategies that you should focus on first. For the things that you are beginner in and are least profitable, you should not even bother starting; you can put this in the trash bin icon on your computer. The priority matrix will help you figure out what to prioritize first in your business.

This exercise will evaluate the risk of implementing these specific strategies. If you know what you are doing and it is most profitable, then you should do it. Investing in a click funnel and producing global Facebook ads could be profitable; however, if you have never done it before, you should take a careful approach because of the financial risk.

Consider joining an established business community so that you can get help and obtain feedback as you create your business offering. Hire a marketing consultant to create a website funnel for you so that it is done right. This will provide you with some insurance to being successful while reducing the risk. It will also give you exposure to a novel audience, including potential clients or potential business partners who you might not have had contact with otherwise.

See Business Plan Worksheets
Appendix H: Strategy Matrix

Step Four: Current and Future States and Risk

This step is probably the most important to creating a clear picture of where you want your business to be in the future and compare it to where it is today. Identify the risks that may get in your way on your business journey. What are the hurdles and pitfalls going to be? It is an exciting journey of discovery ahead of you, so think about the obstacles first before you execute.

Say you are a chiropractor and you want to be a successful public speaker on body health. You want to write a book and become an authority in health and wellness and earn $500,000 per year. You need a clear picture of the destination you want to get to and to map out your journey. If you end up selling your chiropractor practice, you will need to figure out what to do next.

First you want to analyze your current state of affairs and identify your strengths and weaknesses. Complete a SWOT analysis of your current business so that you have a clear picture of what you excel at and a clear picture of the opportunities and challenges on the path forward. You need to understand who your competitors are and what is going to hold you back from achieving your dreams.

Next you need to map out what you want your future business to look like. What is going to be the overall framework of your future business? Are you going to have business coach, accountants, bookkeepers, virtual assistants, marketing, branding, web designers, graphic designers, etc.? Are you going to partner with other business to remove some of the pressure of being an entrepreneur?

If you can make some key partnerships, you can grow faster. As a chiropractor, are there any health and wellness organizations you can partner with? Can you write columns in health magazines or speak at a health summit or expo? Visualize where you want to be in the future. You can map out what you need to implement so that future business can take shape.

You are now going to focus on the risks that will impede you realizing the future state of your business. What limitations do you have? These could be financial or limited resources. It could be that you need to establish a brand and educate yourself on marketing and sales strategies. You need to evaluate any potential risks that could potentially hold your business back.

After you have completed the risk analysis, you should do a gap analysis between where you are today and where you want to be in the future. Then you can look to implement the key elements and strategies you identified during the risk matrix exercise. Your gap analysis may include the functions, processes, organizational structures, knowledge, training, and any other requirements that will help get you from the current to the future state of your business. Now you can clearly define your change strategy and your road to a successful transition.

Step Five: Monitor and Take Action

This stage of our business pivot is where we do the detailed work to monitor requirements for your future business. What is going the be the business flow? Will you require additional staffing? What are the capabilities and roles of future employees (including yourself)? You should define and model how your business is going to work. What are you going to require for your business to function? Will you need a new website or Facebook business account? What will that look like? Are you going to need a computer programmer to set up a membership or functional e-commerce website to generate revenue? Will you need to set up a Shopify website? Will you need additional investors in your company so that you can grow?

Once you have figured out everything that your future business will require, you will need to verify your findings. Will this be feasible strategy to carry out to build your new business, or will there be constraints limiting you? Conduct a beta test on the new software being implemented in your new business. Will you be conducting strategies that are prioritized in accordance with profitability and expertise as discussed in the strategy matrix? Is your process for developing your new business clear, understandable, unambiguous, and concise, or is there further research that you need to do to gain clarity? This verification step is about checking that all your processes and strategies are sound.

After you have verified those details, you need to validate the alignment of your strategy. By alignment, I mean you want to make sure all implementations are consistent with the scope of your business. You do not want to implement strategies that are not going to provide value for your business or key partners. Value is usually profit, but it can also be value for education, community, or personal fulfillment. If you can make the world a better place *and* make money, then the world is your oyster!

You should also consider any assumptions that you are making about the profitability of your future business. Do you have an inspirational message that is going to connect to your customer? Are you making assumptions that your customers are going to buy what you are selling? Recall that you should always be checking in using surveys, research, or reviews to understand your most important key player: **your customer**. If you have made assumptions about your customer's wants, needs, and desires, make sure that you identify this as a risk. Any risks should be evaluated and either reduced, avoided, or eliminated in the future before money is invested.

Another important requirement is the architecture for your business, which you should map out. How are all decisions being made and by whom? How will your customer journey and experience look from point of sale, inventory, delivery, and support? What is your process for refunds or complaints? What is your process for training new staff? Will you need to create training videos? What is the structure of your company? Should you create a *roles and permission matrix* so that every role has clear responsibilities (this could also be used for a new job posting). You want your company to grow organically by hiring generalists. Generalists can take work away from you so that you can focus on the big-picture direction of your business.

Now that you have verified and validated alignment of your business strategies, examined the risks, and defined the architecture of your future business, you are ready to act! Time to start implementing each of the processes you have identified to create your new business strategy.

You can work with your key players to put your business pivot in motion. Hire new contract positions, develop your website or Facebook account, set up a Shopify account or e-commerce platform, start a new marketing and sales strategy, order new software from vendors, or join a new business community to help grow your coaching practice.

You have verified and validated your action plan to be in alignment with your strengths and hired for your weakness. You are implementing the strategies that are going to produce the greatest benefit for you and your business without taking unnecessary risks.

Step Six: Evaluate, Assess, and Explore

As you are putting your plan into action, it is important to continue to evaluate and analyze the results. Continue the cost-benefit analysis of your marketing and sales strategies to reduce unnecessary expenses. Consider using focus groups or survey customers after an event to acquire feedback. Conduct another SWOT analysis as you are working toward the future state of your business.

Are there any new opportunities or threats that have emerged? Seize opportunities! Remove or reduce threats! If you made a bad hiring decision, act rather than letting things fester. These types of pitfalls will have a detrimental effect on you and your business.

Track your key performance indicators (KPIs) so that you know how your business is performing. KPIs should be aligned with your business measures, goals, and objectives. Do you have performance targets for sales? Have you tested your new software application? If you are beta-testing a new platform, what is your target date for release?

You may want to design prototypes or proof of concepts for a new product offering. When collecting performance measures, be mindful of your sample size, frequency, timing, and currency. When you are analyzing your performance measures, check for variances, accuracy, risks, and trends, and compare how your solution performance is aligned with the desired value of the outcome. If you are perplexed by this, consider consulting a business analyst.

Create a business model canvas for your business. This is a way to look at how your business creates, delivers, and captures value from your customers. A business model canvas looks at nine important variables, including key partnerships, key activities, key resources, value proposition, customer relationships, channels, customer segments, cost structure, and revenue streams. Revenue streams can include anything from sales, subscription fees, and transaction or usage fees to lending, renting, or leasing.

If you have a staff team, you should complete a cultural assessment of your business enterprise. Do your key players appreciate the value of your change and accept the solution? Sometimes tenured staff may be resistant to change and uncomfortable with new processes. As a leader, you need to take charge and unite your team around a common vision and mission for your future business.

If there are cultural issues, you may need to hire someone to help with HR or a consultant to determine the underlying causes and create a solution. Your staff may require further training to improve skills to adapt to the new state of affairs. You may also need to adjust your business to staff working from home or hire contract workers.

You finally reach the stage when you have implemented all your chosen strategies and evaluated the results. You need to look at what is going well and what needs improvement. Evaluate the limitations of your change strategy and the limitations of your business itself. Is there anything that requires adjusting? Should you explore some new strategies since the initial ones have been executed? Look to reduce complexity of your processes. Explore tactics to increase efficiency and productivity by eliminating redundancy. Avoid waste by completely removing activities that do not add value or contribute to the final product or service delivery.

Continue to identify new capabilities or opportunities. Try variability of your product or service offering by exploring new avenues or revenue sources. Explore new partnerships that could create new revenue streams. Look at marketing your business through other avenues that are in alignment such as magazines, websites, expos, or business communities. Opportunity cost is missing out on the potential value that could be achieved by pursuing another course of action. Seize these opportunities that present themselves and continue to explore new worlds of abundance!

Risk Lesson from a $25,000 Business Fail

In 2019, I purchased a local referral networking organization for $25,000. I had great dreams of growing this networking group to a unique and high-quality group in my city. I was competing with BNI and two other established networking groups in addition to several other organizations that were building business communities. Altogether, I counted at least seventeen other local networking groups, whether online or in-person, that I would be competing for members with!

I worked with a virtual assistant, and I was focusing on growing the membership by one member per month. I was organizing grand opening events and visitor meetings. I rebranded the business to look hipper, yet I kept some of the fundamental processes intact. I used the membership revenue to improve the branding and marketing, including T-shirts, banner displays for trade shows, and sharp-looking brochures.

But what I did not spend enough time with is understanding the risks of my growth strategy. If you are working with an established organization, any change will either work for you or against you. Initially I had support from four out of the five chapters of my networking group. One chapter immediately jumped ship to another networking club because they had a better web platform. Initially, the other four chapters appeared they were going to support me.

However, it was not a smooth ride! One of the chapters was extremely critical and vocal about everything I did and every change I made. This one was the first pioneer chapter of the club that was created twenty years earlier. I did surveys and acknowledged the feedback I received. Things were going relatively well with most clubs, and I was ready to implement my growth strategy. I started a new club that included a pizza lunch, and we met at a shared coworking space (suitably called Collab Space).

Next, I wanted to start a chapter out on the west end of town where there was a former club that had gone independent. In fact, there were four members of one of my chapters who were also in this club. I organized a grand opening and met with the club a week before to let them know of my intentions. I did get some skepticism but decided to forge on ahead. And that was a fatal mistake. The grand opening went well, but the members of the independent club were irate. Since there were members in both clubs, it poisoned my other chapter. It came to a head when an older, potbellied business owner for an insurance company stood up and read a letter out loud; he basically tore a strip off me. I tried to take it offline, but he insisted on ripping into me with his verbal daggers. In the end, that club went independent, and this downward momentum led to the dissolution of the remaining groups.

I am telling you this story because I killed my business by not identifying the risks of growing too fast, too soon. I would have been more successful if I had kept things the same for two or three years before implementing a growth strategy. I should have communicated more with key players, including the chapter presidents, in all the decision-making processes. However, it was like herding cats to organize a meeting with the clubs (unless I bought them food). Little did I know of the conspiring exit strategy that was going on against me without my knowledge.

Ultimately my mistake was that I was too stubborn. I wanted to achieve my growth objectives even if it meant stepping on the toes of others. But what I did not realize was that these were my own feet and legs I was taking out. Those two legs of the club were the only things holding it together. I would have been better off to work with a business coach or the former business club advisor who could help me understand these risks. But silly me, I was young and inexperienced, thinking it would be a waste of time and money. Lesson learned: understand your risks before you proceed! End of story.

PART 7:
YOUR STRATEGY

16. Get Rich
Make More Money

What is Working Well?

What are your three most profitable sales activities? Are you ready to make more money in your business? Why not focus on the clients and activities generating the most profit for your business? If you are a coach or public speaker, are you making the most money on your speaking tours or coaching sessions? Focus on that which is generating the most revenue for your business. On the flip side, stop wasting time on activities not generating revenue where you feel you are spinning your wheels.

The first year running a networking organization, I focused on promoting member businesses to add value. I was bringing in about one new member per month to my existing clubs. Since each new member was generating the most revenue, I would have been smarter to focus on membership and let the virtual assistant do all the social media marketing.

As a financial advisor, I run several marketing strategies, including seminars (now webinars), center of influences, and networking. I created a top ten list of my highest revenue-generating prospects. This exercise allowed me to focus on those people who are going to make the biggest difference in my business. I also include the marketing strategy in a living business plan so that I can evaluate the success analytics of these various campaigns.

Take time to identify the three most important revenue-generating activities for your business and focus exclusively on them. It is easy to get distracted with other business partnerships and marketing campaigns. By putting your focus on the activities making the most difference in your business, you will amplify your sales.

Underpromise and Overdeliver

Leave your customer wanting more by underpromising and overdelivering. You can exceed their expectations by providing a superior customer service experience. The greatest way to build your business is through word of mouth referrals. Studies show that 85 percent of business is generated this way.

If you deliver the results to your client's expectation, they will be satisfied with the outcome. If you surprise your client with a "wow" experience, you will leave them singing your praise to others for an exceptional job well done. Don't be afraid to ask for a referral after your client has expressed praise for your service. You could say something like: "I love working with people like you. Do you have any friends or family like yourself who you could introduce me to?" You may also try, "Who do you love that I can also help?"

Become a Marketing Superstar

Update your business plan and review the effectiveness of your marketing and sales action items. You want to maintain focus and be accountable to your sales and marketing plan. If you are running online advertisements or public displays, take the time to evaluate the effectiveness of those marketing strategies. You can monitor this by having an accountability partner, whether a business coach or consultant.

Review this at least once per quarter so that you can adapt and change your business plan to the most effective sales and marketing strategies. The definition of insanity is repeating the same thing and expecting different results. Strive to keep your business operating on a sound and level plane. You can do this by constantly evaluating your sales and marketing process by checking in on the effectiveness of your actions. Be adaptable to make changes if your marketing strategies are not bringing in new clients.

Finding a good business coach can make a huge difference in your business. A coach will identify things you do not see and help you identify what is working and what is not. An effective coach will help you create goals for your business and be accountable. A coach is not there to discipline you or make you feel guilty. They are there to help you achieve that which you are striving for to meet your goals. There may be times in your business when you want to take a break from your coach, which is perfectly fine. But when you are ready to hit the ground running, your coach will be there to help you achieve maximum results.

A local website designer won the Top 40 Under 40 award for her business after she worked with a business coach and a mastermind group. She invested over $1,000 per month in her coaching and mastermind group. This investment in herself and her business proved fruitful. She achieved exceptional success in her website business and paid off her mortgage.

Seeing these results of her Top 40 Under 40 award certainly increased her credibility. I approached her myself to inquire about designing a website for one of my businesses. Success breeds more success. The best investment is the investment in yourself. A good coach will help you maximize your potential.

Find a Social Media Mentor

Several marketing gurus can teach you everything about creating a successful online marketing strategy using social media to grow your following. One of the most well-known is Russell Brunson, who popularized click funnels; his company creates landing pages to help sell your products or services online. Mark Lack is an expert on branding from whom you can learn expert branding techniques to grow your social media following with a personal branding blueprint. Anthony and Adrian Morison run the Digital Marketing Academy and teach you how to create and grow your business by creating online courses. Ken Dunn and Nicholas Boothman teach you how to *Write a Saleable Book* in a *Writing Madly Weekend* workshop before you *Publish like a Pro* using the *Authority Factor* marketing strategy. There are several specialists you can find online who have been very successful in specific social media strategies, including Facebook, Instagram, YouTube, Podcasts, LinkedIn, Google, online courses, etc.

You can pay $1,000 to $1,500 to join one of these marketing gurus' social media schools and learn through a guided process. The second option is to choose a DIY method. In this strategy, you can learn how to market yourself online by trial and error and by watching DIY videos. You can join online programs such as Teachable and learn how to create your own online course using the software.

Profit from the Competition

Sometimes it takes time to understand how you stand up against your competition. If this is someone who you admire and look up to for their skills and abilities in branding or marketing, maybe you can learn from them. But you can also look at partnerships where there is a win-win situation. For example, you can approach a potential partner with your initiative and offer to split the profits fifty-fifty. Seek an established entrepreneur with an established network or following; they may will be willing to share your offer if they have something to benefit. This will help you build your brand and credibility by having their endorsement for your business. Identify business owners who have the same audience you are looking for in the field you are looking to make progress in. This could also include magazines, podcasts, seminars, etc. You can use affiliate marketing platforms to structure the revenue streams.

Jay Abraham shared a strategy to search out people who used to work for your competition. If they still have a contact list and no nonsolicitation clause, you could partner with them and monetize their contact list by having direct sales and marketing to them. You can compensate them through results-based performance. If you can partner with someone who can provide leads or sell to new prospects, you can offer a commission that will motivate them to participate with you by benefiting from the sales.

Jay states that you can't profit from your competition or outthink them unless you know them. You should do a SWOT analysis of your competition. You should study the reviews of your competitor and understand what people like or don't like. By correcting issues that your competitor is not doing right or doing more of what people are looking for, you can grow your client base. Why do people buy from them and not from you? What does the market desire, and what are their disappointments? You should examine and reflect upon what you can gain from your competition by studying them and the reviews.

Don't Turn Away Opportunity

Recently I approached a professional carpenter to inquire about building a deck.

However, I had a unique proposition because I wanted to participate in the building process as I was interested in carpentry. Now I realize this may be a tradeperson's worst nightmare to have to work with your customer, but it was something I was excited to do. I even offered clear roles to structure this experiment by having him as the foreman and myself as a worker. I painted the picture for him that he could use the money to take his family on a nice vacation. But he looked uncomfortable and declined my offer. In my reality, he was throwing away an $8,000 opportunity.

If I was in his shoes, I would have embraced the opportunity to get additional revenue for my business. If you are willing to meet someone halfway and get outside your comfort zone, you are destined to be more successful! You can't paint every customer with the same brushstroke. You can have your service and sales practices in place. But always be open to new ideas, new approaches, and new ways of doing things. Or else you should just find a nine-to-five job and do the same thing every day.

I envisioned that this carpenter could create a unique carpenter coaching business. Rather than be like every other carpenter who builds decks and basement renovations, he could have built a unique coaching carpentry practice that helps DIY people like me successfully build a deck. We could have created a DIY video of the deck-building process to help him create a six-figure business!

I came across a salesman who was laid off from his luxury car business because of the pandemic. An idea I had for him was to approach sales managers of other car dealerships. He could offer to sell their vehicles in exchange for a specific commission. Let's say he approaches Mercedes, Audi, and Volvo dealers and arranged to bring in new customers in exchange for a commission. He could become a Luxury Auto Coach—a broker for luxury cars.

He could create an entire car coaching practice and market himself online with tips on how to buy automobiles and things to be aware of with purchasing luxury cars. By thinking outside the box, you will differentiate yourself from your competition and have unlimited success opportunities. By identifying your niche target market and ideal client, you can focus your sales and marketing activities for your perfect client.

17. Take It to the Next Level
Raise the Bar

Catch the Big Fish

In my last sales gig, during my lunch breaks, I enjoyed walking along the local park nature trails by a pond. One day as I reached the pond, there was a large Cormorant perched on a dead, overturned tree. I say large because it resembles the size of a Blue Heron. It sits there and waits for the next fish to swim by before gulping it up. Once your business is off to the races, keep a laser focus on that big fish that may come within your reach. You may miss it sometimes, but when you catch a big fish, it may allow you to jump roads ahead in your business.

Who is that big client you want to attract in your target market? If you could pick anyone in the world to be your next client, who would that be? If you can acquire larger customers, you can work smarter, not harder. Once you have identified the big fish, who will change your life and your business, you can develop a specific marketing strategy geared toward this potential client.

You need to put yourself in their shoes and imagine what it is they want and are looking for in life. What is it that drives them? What do they want more of and what do they desire? Who could you reach out to who personally knows this person? Can you find a third party to make an introduction? It takes more time and strategy to identify those large potential clients and it is a more competitive landscape to acquire them. But the potential gain for your business may be tenfold. If you can visualize and affirm this success, you can realize it with the right efforts, thoughts, and actions. If you can dream it, you can achieve it!

In my last financial firm, I worked myself to the bone, often prospecting to 8 p.m. knocking on doors to build up my client base. I would follow up with five to ten calls, who either did not answer or declined my offer. I would spend thousands of dollars through a seminar firm and end up with zero results.

After that experience, I chose no longer to bang my head against a wall in sales. I decided to start working smarter, not harder. Once I identified my ideal client, I would reflect and spend more time building the rapport and find common ground. I would identify the pain points, provide the a-ha moment, and let them know that they can finally retire. In the end I had to use one-fourth the effort to get twice the results by focusing on what matters and not just being a robotic salesperson.

Be Laser-Focused

You can set up a specific marketing action plan to attract the big fish to your pond. If that is your ideal client, you can set up a specific strategy that will attract a high-value opportunity. Busy CEOs are constantly traveling and spending little time with family. Most successful CEOs struggle with work-life balance. They may desire more quality time with their family or want more recreation time. They may want to give back knowledge based on their huge success. Is there a specific charity they support or a hospital board they are involved with? Wherever there is a will, there is a way; you just need to find it.

The more specific you can be with your target market, the better. By having a specific target market, you can customize your marketing to attract that ideal client. Different demographics have different needs at different life stages. Young couples are usually focused on raising a family and buying their first home. Middle-aged people are advancing in their careers and saving for their child's post-secondary education. Retirees are looking at leisure activities and travel and may be focused on travel or their grandchildren.

At this stage in your business, you should have a target market to devote your business to. Create an ideal client avatar that includes sex, occupation, and income. For example, a target market could be small business entrepreneurs with one to four employees, ages forty to sixty-five, earning $250,000 to $500,000 in revenue.

Here is a strategy I focused on to interview a CEO of a specific publicly traded company.

I had joined a volunteer organization, Kiwanis, that had invited this CEO as a guest speaker. After his talk, I introduced myself to him. I also knew the photographer who had taken the photos for a magazine he was featured in.

Later, I scheduled an interview with another business owner who this former CEO had partnered with in a business venture. After the interview, I provided value by introducing a potential investor for their company. This business owner provided the contact info and even suggested the best time to contact him. I took down this information and on the designated day (Saturday), I sent out an email.

When I emailed him, I referenced his Kiwanis talk that featured him as a guest speaker. After sending out the introduction email, I received a response, and he recollected in amusement that this talk seemed ages ago. He confirmed his willingness to schedule the interview and copied his executive assistant to book the date. After some back and forth, I booked the interview and used his photo in the landing page to promote the event.

I landed an interview with another high-profile, multimillion-aire entrepreneur through an event organizer who had also hosted this celebrity as a keynote speaker. I had a good working relationship with the event organizer, so he trusted me in connecting to the personal assistant. He accepted a thirty-minute slot for the interview and took full advantage in recording it to use for my upcoming event.

If you can do business with a high-quality business owner, it opens the door to more opportunity. A celebrity endorsement adds credibility to your business. What better way to add credibility and branding than working with a high-profile client? You will learn more about what it takes to become successful. By raising your bar, you can open the door to higher-level prospects. Can you guess who multimillionaires hang out with? Well, other millionaires! Improve your network to create the dream business you desire in life.

18. Zen Business
Keep It Simple

Become a Minimalist

This is a good phrase to put up on your wall at home. I see a lot of business owners working ten- or twelve-hour days. They are stressed and it is causing problems in their marriage with their partner. They are launching new projects on a whim and getting stuck when bottlenecks appear.

It is time to simplify your life, my friend. What is it that sparks joy in your life? Is it time to declutter and apply minimalism to your business? Start with your office desk. My guess is that if you are like me, you have papers strewn all over your desk. Maybe you have an email inbox with over one thousand emails. Although geniuses often have cluttered desks (e.g., the absent-minded professor), see how you feel when you have a clean workspace.

Let's start with your email. If you haven't already created email rules for your inbox, it is time to start. First, create folders for all your emails, including finance, marketing, client folders, vendors, coaching, sales, volunteer, etc. After you have created the folders, you can create rules (in Outlook) for incoming emails that automatically put them in all the relevant email folders. I no longer have any emails that appear in my main email box unless they are new. I even have a spam email box for unwanted items and created rules to have emails automatically deleted if I am unable to unsubscribe from a vendor.

Is that email confirmation you received for a lunch meeting one year ago necessary?

Probably not. Next, try deleting at least 75 percent of those emails that are no longer relevant. If there is something important that you want to keep, save the file as a separate document in a separate folder or highlight with a star or exclamation mark next to that email. You can keep the most recent client email or email chain and delete the older stuff that is no longer useful.

After you have decluttered your email inbox, it is time to work on your office space. However, don't be too hard on yourself about having a messy desk. Some say having a messy desk is a sign of creativity and intelligence. But why not organize your papers with physical folders in a filing cabinet. Spend the $30 or $50 it costs to buy a two-level filing cabinet, file folders, and labels from Staples or your local office supplier. Trust me, it will feel so much better to get your office organized and decluttered.

Declutter Your Business

It is now time to apply the decluttering to your business. Look at all the projects and organizations you are involved with and reevaluate the effectiveness they are having in your business. Have you received any referrals in the BNI networking group you joined? BNI stands for Business Networking International; it is a franchised networking organization founded in 1985 by Ivan Misner. If you are paying thousands of dollars per year and are not receiving value from your membership organization, don't waste more money on a membership renewal. However, if you are getting business, enjoy the social aspect or get a free membership as an executive, then do what feels right.

Pick the three most profitable marketing and sales strategies you have in your business and focus on them. If it is not helping your business, it is hurting it. Wouldn't you rather be spending your time with family, friends, or yourself? Stop wasting time with people not helping you or your business. It is time to put you and your business first. It is time to cut ties with those who are only focused on themselves and are not supporting you. You want to spend your time with other positive team players like yourself who will invest time in helping others grow and improve.

Now that you have freed up some time, you should do something that you love. You could take your kids, friend, or spouse out to a nice dinner at a downtown restaurant or patio. Maybe purchase tickets to a movie or local musical. Book that vacation or go for a nature hiking trip you have been dreaming about over the past five years. Get a massage, facial, or a manicure at the local spa. You deserve it for all the hard work you have put into your business and the success you have achieved so far. Reward yourself once you have achieved your goals.

Guess what? After you return to your business all refreshed and rejuvenated, you can start spreading that positive energy. With a positive mindset, the universe will reward you and deals will fall right on your lap. You must fix yourself and recharge your batteries before you can fix your business. This is the primary thing that is holding you back from success. Those who are disciplined and constantly evaluating their business will become successful.

Learn How to Say "No"

The first year or two in your business, you were joining every networking group and volunteer organization and taking any customer who would have a conversation with you. It is time to raise the bar. Start focusing your business on either those clients who are profitable to you or those clients who you want to spend your valuable time with. Spend your time with those who are going to help your mindset and your business become better.

It is time to start saying "No." This past year, I attended a real estate seminar with the number one realtor in my city by sales volume. After the presentation, a couple of business owners asked the realtor to buy her lunch without even saying what the meeting purpose was for. Without batting an eye, she declined the offer. She already knows that most likely this lunch will take up too much of her time she is already spending on her twenty-member team and real estate development companies. After she declined the lunch, the two business owners cut to the chase so she could decide on the offer right away.

Are you a person who accepts anyone who sends you a Facebook friend request? Now that you have deleted 25 percent of the negative energy people, it is also time to decline Facebook friend requests unless you know the person or they can benefit you. Most people are sending you invites because they like your photo, want something from you or for themselves, or they want to be nosey and find more about you. If someone wants to be a fan, they can follow you no problem. Enjoy having lots of followers.

I find it funny to see people with the five thousand Facebook friends. I recently had someone ask me to send them a Facebook request. It wasn't possible to do because their Facebook account was already maxed out. It is time to decline those friend requests.

Do you really want all these strangers knowing about your business? If you want to grow your network, join groups that involve something you are interested in to meet like-minded people. Don't join organizations because you feel you should be networking more.

You need to focus on what will make you most happy so that you can simplify your life and enjoy the fruits of your labor. The happier you are running your business, the more successful your business will become.

Fire Toxic People in Your Life

It is time for you and your business to rise above and shine with all your inner radiance, passion, and joy. But to do so, you need to remove yourself from any toxic relationships killing your inspiration. You are, or will, become like the five people you hang out with.

Look at Elon Musk. He married a business manager. So did Celine Dion, and she became one of the highest paid Vegas singers. By no means am I suggesting firing your spouse. But maybe consider having more "me time" to yourself to recharge your batteries. Take a week off or go on a weekend getaway with your friends, your women's group, or your golf buddies. To achieve your greatest potential, you need to reenergize your batteries.

19. Agree to Succeed
Say "Yes" to Opportunity

Learn When to Say "Yes"

Nick Boothman, author of *How to Make People Like You in 90 Seconds or Less*, was asked by his daughter to speak at a women's networking event. He reluctantly agreed to speak. One person at that event was impressed and requested he speak for a RE/MAX real estate conference. After speaking at the event, he was invited to speak at an international speaking tour, which launched his career as a public speaker.

You never know where things are going to lead to. Trust your gut. If it is something that you feel may open a new door, make a new connection, or create a new opportunity, then why not say "yes." You should only be saying "no" to the same old tired group of poor business owners only concerned with themselves and their own objectives.

Try Something New

What is something different you can do for your business? Have you considered writing a book? Have you considered making educational videos to promote yourself on YouTube? If you are not comfortable on social media, why not teach yourself how to use it properly or hire a marketing professional to assist you?

There are enough DIY videos on YouTube to teach yourself how to do something productive online. You may find things are a lot easier than you thought. One of the big realizations I had was that a Facebook business account can hardly have any views. However, if you create a Facebook group page, all members of that group should see anything that you post. So why are you posting stuff that hardly anyone will even see on a Facebook business page when you can get 80 to 100 percent viewership on your Facebook group page.

Are you on Instagram yet? If you are selling a product and you are not on Instagram, you are missing a lot of opportunity. There is software you can use that will post on multiple social media sites at the same time. Are you familiar with how hashtags work? By adding hashtags to your Instagram posts, they will automatically be posted to your Facebook page, so there is no need to be posting each separately.

Try something that feels uncomfortable to grow. The things you are uncomfortable with are the things that will take you and your business to the next level.

How about doing some public speaking events? Try to find an event that will get you in front of your ideal client. Use your social intelligence to speak to the organizer or event coordinator and ask them to have you at their next speaking engagement. I would suggest this strategy rather than trying to plan your own event because you need to develop your own following. If you do not have a following, you will end up organizing it and only hear crickets at the event.

20. Live the Dream
Have Fun

Focus on What You Love

Y ou have dreamed of starting your business and are finally off to the races. For the time you need to spend on your business, don't you want to do what you enjoy? We need to be honest with ourselves and understand our strengths and weaknesses. You want to do that which you are good at and assign the other tasks to someone else, such as a virtual assistant.

Do the work that you enjoy. Activities you don't like to do may be fun and enjoyable for someone else. It is so important to have fun with your business because enthusiasm is infectious and will help drive your team to greater success.

What do you love to do in your business? Is it meeting with clients or customers? Do you love the creative process of marketing and branding? Are you a numbers person? You will be most happy if you are doing what you love. If you are at the point of running a six-figure business, it is time to consider hiring or contracting work out to other people. You may consider hiring a virtual assistant (VA) or support staff to complete the tasks that you do not enjoy so that you can focus on doing what you love to do!

Outsource the Rest

How about hiring a virtual assistant? How would you like someone managing your calendar and booking your meetings? Would that make life a little easier? Rather than being bombarded with scheduling your own meetings, you could have another person completing those tasks for you. It provides you with a gatekeeper to ensure you are not wasting time meeting with someone not going to benefit your business.

It is time to delegate administration tasks to someone else. There are agencies where you can hire admin oversees, such as 123 Employee or Fiverr. You could hire a local virtual assistant if you want someone more hands-on as your executive assistant. Try to hire to your weakness and hire people who have an X factor. What I mean by X factor is someone with additional useful skills or connections beyond that which they were hired for. You may find a VA who is strong on social media marketing or has a bookkeeping background. You want people who can be generalists and help you on multiple levels, people who can provide additional ideas as you grow and expand your business.

Journey, Not the Destination

It is the journey that counts and not the destination. If you can get to where you are having fun in your dream business, then you are at the ideal place. You want to be energized each morning you start your day in your business. Enjoy challenging yourself and your business to become better than it was yesterday. When it gets to where you are not enjoying the journey, it is time to think of a succession plan to either sell your business or find something new. You have only one life to live, so you should enjoy it and make it count or else find a new destination or journey to explore.

The Vikings did not stay in one place. They ventured on new journeys to England, France, Russia, Iceland, and Newfoundland to find new lands to conquer, settle, and meet new people along the way. They built versatile ships they needed to sail on their journeys along rough seas and narrow canals. They conquered new lands while remaining true to their values and customs. They acquired new wealth and shared the riches with their clan. I love the passion, dedication, and resilience of the Vikings to explore as they were never satisfied with the status quo.

Recharge Your Batteries

When you achieve success in your business, take the time to celebrate. Go out to a movie or a show with your significant other. Go see your favorite band perform or that music festival you have been excited to see. When you achieve your one- or five-year goal, take your family on that dream vacation you have always wanted. Take time to smell the roses and celebrate the success you have worked so hard to achieve.

21. The Bottom Line
To Sum Up

To Recap

We discussed the importance of understanding the top five reasons businesses fail and make sure that you don't fall into any of those traps. We discussed twenty principles to help create your million-dollar business. After reading this book, try to take away and implement at least three things we discussed. You can apply these Business Success Principles to your business to increase your likelihood of success. Become the rockstar business owner you were destined to be!

Next is a summary of what we covered in this book. First you need to have a sound business that adds value—provide something that people want and need. The only way to know for sure is to talk to people and conduct market research. Once you have a solid business or idea, you can create or reexamine your business plan. Your business plan should include your vision and mission statement, which you should revisit every year. You also should define your ideal client and create an avatar, so you know exactly who you are marketing to. You should complete a SWOT analysis and define your strengths, weaknesses, opportunities, and threats.

Once you have defined your business and the current market, you need to create goals for your business. These goals need to be SMART: Specific, Measurable, Achievable, Realistic, and Time-specific. You can use some cost-effective ways to market your business, including social media and Fiverr. You should also know your numbers and understand what your revenue and expenses will be for the previous and upcoming years. If you are not good with numbers, find someone to work with who is.

Next, we focused on building a solid brand that people will know, like, and trust. If customers don't know you, how can they do business with you? If they don't like you or your business, then they are not likely to be repeat customers. Lastly, if you don't establish credibility or trust, then prospects won't have faith in your product or service. You must be able to see your product/service through your customers eyes by tuning into WII-FM. Put yourself in your prospect's shoes and ask the question about your product or service: "What's in it for me?" Ask yourself how you can improve your brand by having a consistent online brand strategy that is clear, consistent, and true to your vision and mission. Review your brand online and your social media accounts.

Once you have your business strategy established, it is important to focus on your mindset and clarify your personal why. To become a successful entrepreneur, you need to have a strong "Why" that will motivate you to be resilient when dealing with adversity. You can use important tools like creating a vision board to obtain clarity on your personal life goals. You can create a wheel of life and rate all areas in your life to ensure you have balance. If you need time to work on your personal life or work through challenges, take time to do this before you take the next steps with your business. First fix yourself, next understand the market, then elevate your business to the next level!

Do you approach all your prospects with the same brushstroke or are you strategic? If you want to be successful in sales, you should examine what type of customer you are dealing with. Is your prospect an Initiator, Direct, Supportive, or Knowledge personality? The personality type of your prospect should determine the type of strategic approach you take to have a successful buyer's journey.

You should develop your one-minute Presentation (OMP). Think of the *OMP Burger* when you create your elevator pitch. The bottom bun states the problem your prospect is facing, the meat is your value proposition, and the top bun discusses your unique approach to solving the problem your prospect is facing. You should also add your pickle by coming up with an attractive tagline so your prospects will remember you.

Ultimately your success in selling your product or service depends on how effective you are in building relationships. You can build relationships fast and efficiently by practicing the five Cs: find Common ground, have a Conversation that is mindful, use Candid humor, show you Care, and remember to Compliment.

The next step as your business starts to grow is to build a strong team. You want to hire to your weakness and find generalists who are capable of filling in the gaps. Start with hiring a virtual assistant to help with the administration tasks. You may consider hiring a bookkeeper to keep your finances on track. You want to maximize your time and have an efficient, time-blocked calendar. You should focus on the right activities that will drive your business.

Be mindful of who you are spending your time with. Eliminate the negative people who are toxic in your life. Spend time with other successful entrepreneurs with whom you can network, find inspiration, and come up with new marketing ideas. Consider joining a mastermind group and revisit your current networking groups to make sure you a receiving a return on investment.

We examined how to pivot your business while remaining profitable. To elevate your business, you should follow these six steps used by business analysts and Fortune 500 companies. Step 1. Plan the framework for execution by planning your plan. Step 2. Outreach and collaboration with key players so you understand the needs of your stakeholders. Step 3. Understand the key elements and prioritize them using a strategy matrix. Step 4. Current and future states and risk; you need to define your current state and future state and understand the risks. Step 5. Monitor and take action by understanding your business architecture and flow. Step 6. Evaluate, assess, and explore by monitoring important business metrics.

Examine further strategies to elevate your business to the next level. Focus your approach on the top three marketing strategies that are driving your sales. Consider hiring a business coach, join a mastermind to keep your ideas fresh, and hold yourself accountable. Consider working with a social media expert and make sure you capitalize on all opportunities. Examine your competition for new ideas and competitive advantages.

Raise the bar in your business by developing a new strategy to target large business opportunities. Be laser-focused on your approach and carefully plan out your action strategy. Keep it simple by running a Zen business; use minimalism in your office. Declutter your emails and your office space. Consider cropping your social media contacts to increase focus and reduce distractions.

Say "yes" to opportunity by keeping your antennae up for new business fortunes. Try something new like creating promotional or educational YouTube videos or public speaking. Focus on having fun in your business by doing things you love. Take time to recharge your batteries and celebrate your successes.

Next Steps

You know what you must accomplish, and it is time for execution. Congratulations for reading this book to the end and learning about new strategies, tactics, and ideas from the twenty principles we discussed. If you are inspired right now, don't put this book away without using some of these tools. Try to implement at least three to five of these principles right away to elevate your business to the next level.

You started your business with 10 percent inspiration and 90 percent perspiration. It is now time to work more on your inspiration by protecting your mental health. Surround yourself with the right people to make it happen. Sixty percent of your time should be spent on building and fostering those relationships that will help you succeed.

In the first two years, you have put your blood, sweat, and tears to get you where you are today. Now it is time to focus on what is working right and to do more of that. You need to clean up all the extra stuff getting in your way. By focusing on the things working right, you will avoid the other things holding you back.

The most successful millionaires are not out there boasting or telling everyone how great they are. They arrived where they are today through hard work, focus, and resilience. They have exceled at building relationships with other people who have helped them on their journey. They can say "no" to distractions that do not add value to their own business or benefit them. The art of building a successful business is to focus on the things that will make your business more successful and remove the obstacles getting in your way.

Stay humble and focused. Build and foster new relationships with like-minded people; those who are growth-oriented and have a positive attitude on life. You are looking for the 1 percent of people who are there to support you and happy to see you succeed. This quality is rare, but I am sure you can find them. Look for others who you can collaborate with where there is a win-win scenario and you both benefit from referring business or providing introductions. You can establish affiliate relationships where you can receive passive income by referring people to other businesses you support. You can learn how to make money work for you passively by investing and setting up affiliate marketing strategies.

So, listen up, Superstar, you can do this! Get your business unstuck and launch it for success! If you need help, feel free to contact me for support, advice, or coaching. Together we will help you take your business to the next level. This higher level of vibration is where you can think and believe; be the successful entrepreneur you are destined to become!

Own your truth and live your dream!

BUSINESS PLAN
WORKSHEETS

APPENDIX A
MISSION, VISION & IDEAL CLIENT

3 Words that describe the essence of my business?

1. _____

2. _____

3. _____

1. **Mission Statement:** _____

_____

_____

2. **Vision Statement:** _____

_____

_____

3. **Your Unique Value:** _____

_____

_____

4. **Ideal Client:** _____

_____

_____

5. **Marketing to Ideal Client:** _____

_____

_____

APPENDIX B
S.W.O.T ANALYSIS

Strengths: _____

_____

_____

_____

Weaknesses: _____

_____

_____

_____

Opportunities: _____

_____

_____

_____

Threats: _____

_____

_____

_____

APPENDIX C
S.M.A.R.T. GOALS

Specific, Measurable, Achievable, Relevant, Time-framed (S.M.A.R.T.) Goals

Specific: _____

_____

_____

Measurable: _____

_____

_____

_____

Acheivable: _____

_____

_____

_____

Relavent: _____

_____

_____

_____

Time-Framed: _____

_____

_____

_____

S.M.A.R.T. Goal: _____

_____

_____

_____

APPENDIX D
BUSINESS NUMBERS

What are my business numbers?

Income for last fiscal year: $_____   *How can I increase my income?*

(less)

Expenses for last fiscal year: $_____   *How can I reduce my expenses?*

(equals)

Revenue for last fiscal year: $_____   *How can I grow my revenue for next year?*

What business revenue can I achieve for next year?

How much can I increase income by each year: (ex. 5%, 10%, 15%, 20%, 25%)?   _____%

How much can I reduce in my expenses for next year?   _____%

What are my expenses as a percentage of income (i.e., cost of goods sold)   _____%

What is my expense budget for next year?

Marketing $_____

Bookkeeping/Accounting $_____

Self-Improvement/Coaching $_____

Staff $_____

Rent $_____

Utilities/Maintenance $_____

APPENDIX E
20 YEAR REVENUE GOAL

1. $ _____
2. $ _____
3. $ _____
4. $ _____
5. $ _____
6. $ _____
7. $ _____
8. $ _____
9. $ _____
10. $ _____
11. $ _____
12. $ _____
13. $ _____
14. $ _____
15. $ _____
16. $ _____
17. $ _____
18. $ _____
19. $ _____
20. $ _____

APPENDIX F
VISION BOARD

5 YEAR GOAL

INSPIRATION WORD

20 YEAR GOAL

INSPIRATION WORD

GROUNDING IMAGE

INSPIRATION WORD

1 YEAR GOAL

INSPIRATION WORD

LEGACY IMAGE

INSPIRATION WORD

APPENDIX G

ONE MINUTE PRESENTATION BURGER

TOP BUN

How you have a unique process to solving the problem of your prospect.

PICKLE

Your TAG line to make your business memorable.

MEAT

WHAT is the unique value about you and your business product or service.

BOTTOM BUN

Start with a WHY statement of the problem that your prospect is facing.

WHY statement of the problem (bottom bun)? _____

_____

_____

WHAT unique value of your business (meat): _____

_____

_____

TAG line to make your business memorable (pickle):

_____

_____

HOW do you solve the problem (top bun): _____

_____

_____

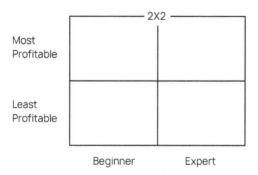

APPENDIX H
STRATEGY MATRIX

2X2

	Beginner	Expert
Most Profitable		
Least Profitable		

3X3

	Beginner	Intermediate	Expert
Most Profitable			
Somewhat Profitable			
Least Profitable			

About the Author

A long with running a networking business, Paul has interviewed hundreds of successful business owners to understand the most important strategies to become successful. As a tenured business owner, Paul Arnold has built six separate businesses in the financial services. His last business was six figures within two years. Paul has over thirty years of sales and marketing experience

Outside of the business world, Paul Arnold is a professionally trained musician and composer/conductor who performs classical guitar, piano and cello. He provides piano and guitar performances for his local church. He lives with his wife and two daughters in Ottawa, Canada.

References

Chapter 2:

Color Infusion. "The Importance of a Vision and Mission Statement." Colourinfusion.ca. February 17, 2017. https://colourinfusion.ca/the-importance-of-vision-and-mission-statements/

Chapter 3:

Lori Hubbard, "Why Is Identifying the Target Market so Important to a Company?"

Last modified February 19, 2019. https://smallbusiness.chron.com/identifying-target-market-important-company-76792.html

Chapter 4:

Kiely Kuligowski, "Why you Need a SWOT Analysis for Your Business." Last modified May 6, 2020. www.business.com/articles/swot-analysis-for-small-business-planning/

Chapter 5:

Mind Tools Content Team, "SMART Goals: How to Make Your Goals Achievable." Mindtools.com. https://www.mindtools.com/pages/article/smart-goals.htm

Chapter 6:

Asheech Advani, "How to Forecast Revenue and Growth." https://www.entrepreneur.com/article/76418

Chapter 7:

Erin Roberts, "Branding: Know, Like and Trust." Last modified January 3, 2020. https://creativeiq.net/branding-know-like-trust/

Chapter 8:

Shama Hyder, "Five Ways to Build A Strong Online Presence for Your Brand." Last modified March 4, 2019. https://www.forbes.com/sites/forbeslacouncil/2019/03/04/five-ways-to-build-a-strongonline-presence-for-your-brand

Chapter 9:

Krista Dickson, "4 Steps to Manifest Your Dream Business." Last modified July 2018. https://elleymae.com/blog-tips/manifest-your-dream-business/

Chapter 10:

Matt Valentine, "The Benefits of Creating a Vision Board." Last modified September 14, 2018. www.goalcast.com/2018/09/14/creating-a-vision-board/

Chapter 11:

Aga Frost, "How to Sell to 4 Different Personality Types." Last modified February 26, 2018. https://blog.hubspot.com/sales/how-to-sell-to-different-personality-types

Chapter 12:

Allison Doyle, "How to Create an Elevator Pitch with Examples." Last modified December 9, 2019. https://www.thebalancecareers.com/elevator-speech-examples-and-writing-tips2061976

Chapter 15:

A Guide to the Business Analysis Body of Knowledge, version 3 (Toronto, Ontario, Canada: International Institute of Business Analysis, 2015).

A free ebook edition
is available with the
purchase of this book.

To claim your free ebook edition:

1. Visit MorganJamesBOGO.com
2. Sign your name CLEARLY in the space
3. Complete the form and submit a photo of the entire copyright page
4. You or your friend can download the ebook to your preferred device

A **FREE** ebook edition is available for you
or a friend with the purchase of this print book.

CLEARLY SIGN YOUR NAME ABOVE

Instructions to claim your free ebook edition:
1. Visit MorganJamesBOGO.com
2. Sign your name CLEARLY in the space above
3. Complete the form and submit a photo of this entire page
4. You or your friend can download the ebook to your preferred device

Print & Digital Together Forever.

Snap a photo

Free ebook

Read anywhere

9 781631 957949